W9-BKK-223

MAKERS OF AMERICA

CHIEF JOSEPH
AND THE
NEZ PERCÉS

ROBERT A. SCOTT

Facts On File
New York

Chief Joseph and the Nez Percés

Copyright © 1993 by Robert A. Scott

Facts On File, Inc.
460 Park Avenue South
New York NY 10016
USA

Library of Congress Cataloging-in-Publication Data

Scott, Robert Alan.
    Chief Joseph and the Nez Percés / [Robert A. Scott].
      p. cm. — (Makers of America)
    Includes bibliographical references and index.
    Summary: A biography of the nineteenth-century Nez Percé chief, concentrating on his unending struggle to win peace and equality for his people.
    ISBN 0-8160-2475-8
    1. Joseph, Nez Percé Chief, 1840–1904. 2. Nez Percé Indians—Biography. 3. Nez Percé Indians—History. [1. Joseph, Nez Percé Chief, 1840–1904. 2. Nez Percé Indians—Biography. 3. Indians of North America—Biography.] I. Title. II Series: Makers of America (Facts On File, Inc.)
    E99.N5J674 1993
    979.004'97402—dc20
    [B]   92-15885

A British CIP catalogue record for this book is available from the British Library.

Facts On File books are available at special discounts when purchased in bulk quantities for businesses, associations, institutions or sales promotions. Please call our Special Sales Department in New York at 212/683-2244 (dial 800/322-8755 except in NY, AK or HI) or in Oxford at 865/728399.

Text design by Debbie Glasserman
Jacket design by Duane Stapp
Composition by Facts On File, Inc.
Cartography by Una Dora Copley
Manufactured by R.R. Donnelley & Sons, Inc.
Printed in the United States of America

10 9 8 7 6 5 4 3 2 1

This book is printed on acid-free paper.

In memory of
Mary Winifred Gibney

Take a good look at me! I will give you my power; what I have got. You may think I am nothing! You may think I am only bones! But I am alive!

—words of a spirit in the vision of a Nez Percé child

CONTENTS

PREFACE

Five hundred years ago, with the arrival of Columbus in the Caribbean, an epic struggle by native peoples of North and South America began. They faced the development and growth of technologically powerful but wasteful and destructive societies throughout both continents. Generations of Native Americans searched for ways to stop the invasion, to avoid it, to understand, to use and to mold it.

The Nez Percé people, living in the vast and isolated plateau of the Pacific Northwest, were among the last groups in North America to face the strange, seemingly invincible culture that called itself "civilization." Theirs was an adaptive, dynamic society that responded creatively to the challenge. But, as with many other Native American groups, freedom for the Nez Percés finally ended with a series of tragic and bloody acts committed under the banner of the United States.

One of the tribe's leaders, Chief Joseph, emerged from this conflict as a mythic figure in American history. He was supposedly the noble champion of a lost cause, a unique and solitary genius whose presence explained the ability of the Nez Percé warriors to humble a modern army until they were finally worn down and overwhelmed. This myth shrouded Joseph years before his death and hides him still. In battle the man was much smaller than this, but in other ways he was greater. Today, on the 500th anniversary of Columbus's arrival, it is time to look at Joseph's place in the confrontation that began in 1492 and that has continued to this day.

This book tries to focus on the man, insofar as possible using the words of people who witnessed his life and times, and to suggest why this life may have meaning for us now. A great deal of information that we normally expect to find about important figures in our history remains unknown in Joseph's case. Some may yet come to light; much of it never will.

But the broad strokes of Joseph's story are clear. He and other great chiefs, the warriors and all the people carried out the creative and tenacious response of the embattled Nez Percé bands to the assaults of the U.S. Army.

Equally or perhaps more important was the course Chief Joseph charted before and after the bloodletting. If we look beyond the myth and the tragedy, we see a quest for a path of enduring struggle and hope—for his and for other peoples—for land, life and freedom. This he followed relentlessly to his last day, defying the campaign of repression that closed in on Native Americans in the late 19th century.

— ROBERT A. SCOTT
May 1992

ACKNOWLEDGMENTS

Many friends and kind strangers have helped me in this project.

Robert Killoran joined me for the drive west from Worcester, Massachusetts, in the summer of 1990. He has helped in innumerable ways since. Elizabeth Hughes met us in the Northwest and devoted herself to helping with research. She also lured her sister, Allison, and Gregory Hagopian into the region, where they helped in a brief but intensive search at the Washington State University Library in Pullman. A third of the intrepid Hughes sisters, Victoria, obtained photographs.

For their kindness and encouragement in brief contacts with me I thank Alvin Josephy and Grace Bartlett. I am most grateful to Bridgett and Michael Welch for taking Robert Killoran and myself into their home near Arlee, Montana, and for the invaluable perspective they shared with us from Michael's years of work among western Native Americans. Thanks also to: John and Dorene Welch; Otis Halfmoon; Betsy Hannula and the Historical Society of Westminster, Massachusetts, home of Nelson Miles; Christine Dunshee; Rocky Blount; and the Worcester, Mass. Public Library.

The papers of Alvin Josephy at the University of Oregon in Eugene are an important resource for Nez Percé studies. Josephy spent many years in research, gathering documents from far-flung sources—some of which are no longer available elsewhere. I am grateful to Fraser Cocks, the curator of special collections at the university's Knight Library.

The papers of Professor Edmond S. Meany at the Washington University Archives in Seattle are a crucial source of information on Joseph. Meany interviewed the chief and queried him by letter on many points. Fortunately M. Gidley published much of this material in his book *Kopet*. But Meany's papers include many other documents the professor acquired in his own research. For guiding me into this voluminous collection I thank Gary Ludell, archives specialist.

Virtually all the Nez Percé narratives that L. V. McWhorter collected were published in his two books. But the McWhorter collection, at Washington State University in Pullman, includes a great deal of other material, including fragments of Joseph's personal life and McWhorter's correspondence with Yellow Wolf, other Nez Percés and people who had met Joseph. Archivist Jose L. Vargas and historical photograph curator Carol Lichtenberg were most helpful.

Thanks are due to Paul Scaramazza for his rigorous yet restrained copyediting of this manuscript.

Finally I thank my parents Tony and Maria Scott, who provided work and living space when the power failed at my home, and my editors, Tony Scott and Nicole Bowen, who were most kind and wise in the face of other failings.

Grateful acknowledgment is given for permission from copyright holders to quote passages from the following:

Days with Chief Joseph, by Erskine Wood. Copyright © the Oregon Historical Society, 1970.

An Army Doctor's Wife on the Frontier, by Emily McCorcke FitzGerald, edited by Abe Laufe, by permission of the University of Pittsburgh Press. Copyright © 1962 by University of Pittsburgh Press.

Yellow Wolf: His Own Story and *Hear Me, My Chiefs! Nez Perce History and Legend*, both by L. V. McWhorter; by permission of The Caxton Printers, Ltd., Caldwell, Idaho.

Adventures in Geyser Land, by Frank Carpenter, Hester Guie and L. V. McWhorter; by permission of The Caxton Printers, Ltd., Caldwell, Idaho.

1

ACROSS THE GREAT DIVIDE
August 9, 1877

Colonel John Gibbon knew he had found Nez Percés when he broke out of the forest and saw thousands of horses grazing on a steep slope under the stars. The dark hours of early morning were moonless, clear and cold on that mountainside 7,000 feet above sea level, just east of the Continental Divide. The Nez Percés were far from home but easy to recognize as they slept at the foot of the mountain, in the Big Hole Valley of western Montana. No one else would have so many fine horses.

They were horse breeders, horse herders, trainers and traders, as skilled as any in North America. Their steeds were "lofty, elegantly formed, active and durable," wrote Meriwether Lewis, who in 1805 was part of the first expedition of U.S. explorers to reach the tribe.

Their most outspoken leader, Chief Joseph, was rapidly becoming a famous man. He headed a band from the Wallowa country, in the northeast corner of Oregon state. In council with the whites he had unmasked and defied their belief in racial superiority with the same keenness that Nez Percé rifles would later cut down attacking soldiers. "Perhaps," the chief told one condescending group he dealt with, "you think the Creator sent you here to dispose of us . . ."

He was massive, calm and, as a reporter wrote, "a splendid looking man. He is fully six feet high; in the prime of life—about 35, has a splendid face and well formed head. His forehead is high, his eyes bright yet kind, his nose finely cut . . ." When the army went after four Nez Percé bands, including Joseph's, in June of 1877, many observers agreed there could be but one mastermind behind such audacious peace and wartime resis-

1

tance. They did not as yet comprehend the power and resource-fulness of the Nez Percés.

Long, long ago, bands of the People, as they sometimes called themselves, had made their homes in the Pacific Northwest, where the lower Snake River flows north through a great plateau between the Rocky and the Cascade mountains. This land is 10,000 square miles of rumpled, deeply furrowed earth—mountain ranges crowding into canyons, ravines, high prairies and rolling hills.

About a century before Lewis and Clark came to them, the Nez Percés obtained their first horses from tribes to the south, who in turn had gotten horses from the Spanish. The wide pastures of the Nez Percés' country nourished large herds, while deep river gorges and line after line of mountain barriers protected them from invaders. Here the scattered, river dwell-ing Nez Percé bands became one of the great mounted peoples of the West. The horse gave them a mobility and wealth that they had never known. They ranged across their land and far beyond to hunt, fish, gather wild foods and to trade.

Along with other mounted peoples of the plateau, the Nez Percés created an overland link between the Columbia and Snake river system in the west and the headwaters of the Missouri in the east, extending a network of trade relations among Native American groups from the Pacific to the Missis-sippi River.

Lewis and his partner William Clark followed one Nez Percé route, the Lolo Trail, through the Bitterroot chain of the Rocky Mountains on their pioneering trip into the Northwest interior. Like others who followed them, they were starving and nearly lost when they reached the mountains to the homeland of the Nez Percés in what is today the panhandle of Idaho. And, like the others, they were fed, sheltered and guided through the land by the proud and friendly people. As representatives of their young nation, the explorers exchanged solemn pledges of friendship with the tribe, pledges that generations of Nez Percés remembered and observed.

Like Lewis and Clark, John Gibbon was an officer of the United States Army. He had graduated from West Point, served in the Civil War, and went to a courthouse in Appomat-tox, Virginia, with Ulysses S. Grant to meet Robert E. Lee and arrange the surrender of the Confederacy. Gibbon knew the story of Lewis and Clark well. As he labored up the steep western slope of the divide in pursuit of the Nez Percés, it occurred to him more than once that he was traveling along the route those explorers had taken as they returned eastward through the mountains in 1806.

Gibbon had read their journals, where Clark wrote that the Nez Percés had "shown much greater acts of hospitality than we have witnessed from any nation or tribe since we have passed the Rocky Mountains . . . be it spoken to their immortal honor . . ." Another army officer who visited them in the 1830s said they were "more like a nation of saints than a horde of savages."

Gibbon came not to honor Nez Percés but to see them, as he put it, "slaughtered." He viewed them as animals, part of a race, he later wrote, that "must give way, and disappear." Gibbon had seen the bodies of George A. Custer and his men where the Sioux had left them in June of 1876, by the Little Bighorn River in southeastern Montana. The following winter, he had fought in the Great Sioux War, which broke the power of that huge tribe.

Then, in July 1877, as the four embattled Nez Percé bands headed east into the mountains to escape war in Idaho, Gibbon received orders to stop them before they could reach the plains and possibly inspire the Sioux to rise again.

The colonel had gathered all the men he could and rushed from the north to catch up with the Nez Percés in a forced march of more than 250 miles. The bands, which had carefully avoided trouble as they passed defenseless Montana settlements, did not plan to resume fighting if they could avoid it. They did not realize that soldiers were near. They continued east across the Great Divide and into the Big Hole Valley, a 50-by-25 mile gap in the ranks of towering ridges, where the fingers of the Missouri River system reach their westernmost limit. There the bands stopped to rest and cut tipi poles as Gibbon closed in along their trail.

The colonel and nearly 200 men approached quietly in the darkness, moving east down the mountain slope toward a branch of the Big Hole River that flows northward through grassland and willow thickets. Beyond the stream and roughly parallel to it they could see lines of campfires where about 750 people lay in long lines of tipis. Among them were fewer than

200 men of fighting age, no more than 125 of them actually warriors. The rest were women, children and old people.

"As we halted abreast of the camp the cries of babies and the tone of conversation between the adults could be distinctly heard," Gibbon recalled later. ". . . Their tipis, with their women and children, most of them asleep, were lying almost at our feet."

He did not understand that he was marching his men against a group of mounted hunters who had mastered the use of the white man's best guns. He thought surprise and overwhelming firepower would do the job. Gibbon spread his men out in a long line facing about 80 tipis across the stream. Most of the men carried deadly, fast firing Springfield rifles. Each man had 90 cartridges.

They watched as women emerged from the tipis, piled wood on the fires and returned to their blankets. The colonel passed word down the line to "aim low in firing at the lodges" when the time for shooting came, so as to hit the people lying inside. As they waited in the cold for dawn, some of the men drank whiskey from canteens. Among the 25 or so citizen volunteers who had joined the army troops under Gibbon's command, someone wondered what to do with prisoners. Captain John B. Catlin, leader of the volunteers, brought the answer back to his men: no prisoners. "Boys," the captain whispered, "you know what to do now."

As the first light cut the blackness of the nighttime sky, Natalekin got up and rode out from camp to check on the horses. He was a chief of the Palouse people, relatives and neighbors of the Nez Percés from the Northwest plateau. A few of them had been visiting a Nez Percé band when the army attacked, and they were caught up in the war. Natalekin crossed the stream as the white men moved in and had practically reached them when he leaned forward, peering into the half-light. He was very old and could hardly see. He was unarmed. Four men leveled their guns. "They shot him down," Joseph remembered years later, "like a coyote."

Then all the soldiers fired three times, scything the tipis with lead. They cheered, and charged across the stream. Gibbon watched them go "up the opposite bank, shooting down the startled Indians as they rushed from their tents pell-mell, men, women and children together."

"Bullets were like hail on the camp," a Nez Percé child remembered many years later as an adult. ". . . I heard bullets ripping the tipi walls, pattering like raindrops." Another child recalled a desperate scramble past blazing guns. "It was like spurts of fire, lightning all around."

Some of the people got past the soldiers to seek shelter in the willows or beneath the banks of the stream. Some ran north or south from either end of the camp and then moved around the soldiers to the stream. Others ran east into the open flat land of the valley and dropped into small depressions or any other shelter they could find.

A young woman hid beneath some willows. "A little girl lay close, my arm over her. Bullets cut twigs down on us like rain. The little girl was killed. Killed under my arm."

A boy reached shelter among some stones, then looked back in terror as the attackers took the southern half of the camp. "The soldiers seemed [to be] shooting everywhere," he said, "through tipis and wherever they saw Indians. I saw little children killed and men fall before bullets coming like rain."

Most of the Nez Percés killed that day died in this opening assault. Some soldiers killed women and children deliberately—even a newborn infant and its mother. They set fire to several tipis and burned the children inside to death. They fired on women and children in the stream. Blood colored the water.

Most of the Nez Percé men who died fell trying desperately to hold the soldiers back from the tipis, and the children remaining inside. At least two women, one of them already badly wounded, seized guns from the hands of dying men and fought and died beside them at the tipis. One of these women killed the officer who led the charge against the northern end of the camp. His men became disorganized, and two or three Nez Percés with guns held them back. These soldiers moved south and joined the assault there.

Joseph clutched his six-week old daughter as he fled from a tipi near the stream and dove for the willows. He had no gun and wore nothing but the long shirt he had been sleeping in. He met a warrior by the stream and pleaded for a gun. "Skip for your life," the man answered. "Without the gun you can do nothing. Save the child!" Soon Joseph found someone to take the baby, and he dashed up the mountainside to the milling horses. He mounted and drove the herd away from the fighting.

As tipis burned and screams of children and shouts of soldiers filled the air, the voices of war leaders rose above the sounds, calling to the dazed and scattered Nez Percé men.

> My brothers. Our tipis are on fire. Make resistance! You are here for that purpose!
> Why are we retreating? . . . Shall we run to the mountains and let these white dogs kill our women and children before our eyes? It is better that we should be killed fighting. Now is our time to fight. . . . Fight! Shoot them down!

A few men with guns moved away from the camp and began to pick soldiers off from long range. Yellow Wolf, Joseph's 20-year-old nephew, fought with only a club among the willows by the river. He beat a soldier to the ground and took his rifle. Then, responding to the pleas of the war leaders, he joined a small group of men in a furious counterattack on the southern half of the camp.

"Only about ten brave warriors made here a desperate stand . . . ," he said. "Some had already mounted horses and were fighting, scattered. Others were in the willows fighting. I joined to save the tipis . . . From all sides we mixed them up. I made an advance against some soldiers, got close enough to take good aimed shots. Three of those same enemies went down. I rushed in, took guns and cartridges."

Gibbon's men turned their attention from the tipis and charged back and forth through the willows trying to clear the Nez Percé men from the river. But, the colonel wrote, "as fast as they were driven out in front others would appear in the rear . . . shots soon came pouring into us from all directions" as more Nez Percés found guns. Gibbon himself took a bullet in the buttocks. At sunrise he ordered a retreat back across the river to a wooded knoll north of the camp. "It's another Custer Massacre," a panicking soldier shouted. "Let's get out of here!"

Gibbon was able to keep his men in order and drag most of his wounded with him as warriors pressed after them. Soon the white men desperately dug trenches and piled logs at the crest of the knoll. Their wounded cried and burned their wounds with gunpowder to stop the flowing blood. A few warriors pinned them down as the rest of the Nez Percés returned to the camp.

A toddler stepped up from the river bank, leaving the body of his older brother, who had taken him there to hide. He gazed at the scene, as he remembered years later, innocent and uncomprehending. "In the wrecked camp I saw and heard lots of Indian men and women crying. Oh, lots of them crying. Crying loud, mournful. I could not understand. I did not know. I saw many soldiers, many Indian men and oh, so many women and children lying on the ground. I wondered if they were sleeping so. Later I understood."

The trapped men on the knoll listened and watched as the Nez Percés mourned about 90 dead, two-thirds of whom were women and children. More than four decades later Gibbon wrote how well he remembered the sound. Some of the soldiers told later of women or children they had killed. Some said it was justified because women and even some older children had resisted the assault. Some said only a few of the men had done this killing.

Images of that day haunted Sergeant Charles N. Loynes the rest of his life, especially one of a baby, mangled but still alive, crying and struggling as it lay on the still form of a woman near a tipi. "When I think of these terrible scenes, wrongs waged against human beings, I say, 'Shame! Shame!'" he wrote as an old man. "This great Christian government had power to do differently by those truly patriotic people. It is such remembrances which touch my emotions, and I am led to marvel at the term 'civilization.'"

The reality of the government's policy was now painfully clear to the Nez Percé survivors. They had thought before that the U.S. Army was fighting to drive them from their land and that, by giving up their homes and avoiding trouble with whites in Montana, they had ended the conflict. Joseph and the other chiefs had hoped to renew contact with the government, make a peace that would give them a home. But the very existence of free Indians was intolerable to the government now, let alone the idea of negotiating with them.

The bands had many wounded, but they had to move quickly. More soldiers would surely come. Joseph drove the horses into camp and worked desperately to help the people regain the mobility that was now their only hope. They used their long tipi poles to make travois—long, V-shaped frames each with the narrow end lashed to a horse at the shoulders and the wide

HOMELAND OF THE NEZ PERCÉS

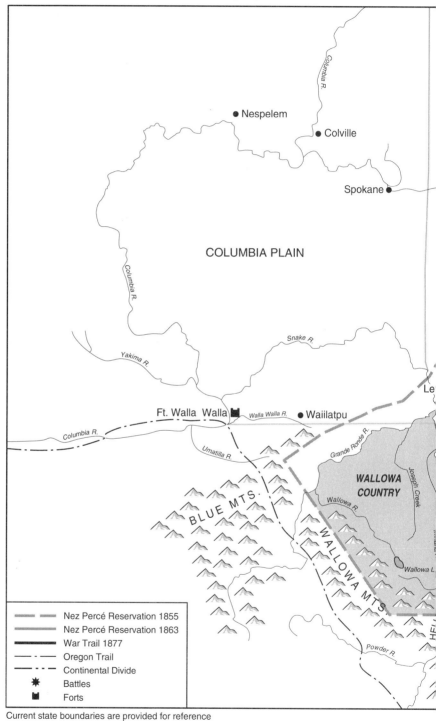

Nespelem

Colville

Spokane

COLUMBIA PLAIN

Columbia R.

Columbia R.

Snake R.

Yakima R.

Le

Ft. Walla Walla Walla Walla R. Waiilatpu

Columbia R.

Umatilla R.

Grande Ronde R.

Joseph Creek

WALLOWA
COUNTRY

Wallowa R.

BLUE MTS.

W
A
L
L
O
W
A
MTS.

Wallowa L.

HF

Powder R.

	Nez Percé Reservation 1855
	Nez Percé Reservation 1863
	War Trail 1877
	Oregon Trail
	Continental Divide
✹	Battles
▉	Forts

Current state boundaries are provided for reference

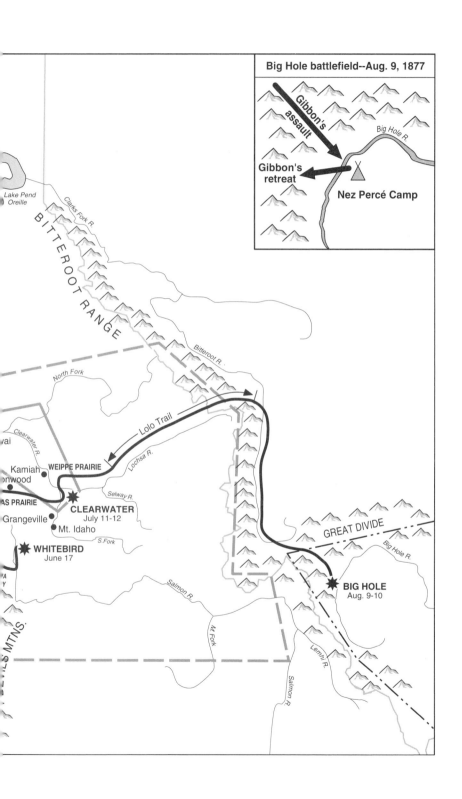

Big Hole battlefield--Aug. 9, 1877

Gibbon's assault

Big Hole R.

Gibbon's retreat

Nez Percé Camp

Lake Pend Oreille

Clarks Fork R.

BITTERROOT RANGE

Bitterroot R.

North Fork

Lolo Trail

Clearwater R.

vai

Kamiah

nwood

WEIPPE PRAIRIE

Lochsa R.

AS PRAIRIE

Grangeville

Mt. Idaho

CLEARWATER
July 11-12

Selway R.

S.Fork

GREAT DIVIDE

Big Hole R.

WHITEBIRD
June 17

Salmon R.

BIG HOLE
Aug. 9-10

M. Fork

LLS MTNS.

Lemhi R.

Salmon R.

end dragged over the ground behind. They stretched hides across the poles behind the horses and strapped on the most seriously wounded. They tied other wounded into the saddle. The dead were wrapped in buffalo robes and buried quickly under the river banks.

Soon after the soldiers were driven off that morning, a long and sorrowing procession straggled south down the valley, as warriors spread out in all directions on horseback, searching for more of the enemy. They found and routed a small detachment on its way to Gibbon's relief and captured a cannon and thousands of rifle cartridges.

Around midday Joseph left to go with the families. In the coming weeks he would be their guardian, helping them move at a brutal pace while doing what they could for the wounded, burying the dead, cooking food, looking after children and caring for that vital and slowly dwindling reserve of strength, the horses. Ollokot, Joseph's younger brother and leader of the Wallowa warriors, stayed behind with some of the men to make sure Gibbon did not follow the retreating families. Like any Nez Percé war leader, he went in front—hugging the ground in a hollow almost at the edge of the soldiers' trenches. With the most experienced fighters now dead, Ollokot and a handful of other fighting leaders were left with no more than 100 warriors to face the converging columns of the army.

These brothers, Joseph and Ollokot, were born and raised in the beautiful Wallowa country, the land of winding waters that rises like a green island from the great plateau of the Pacific Northwest. Mountains, which catch rain and snow, rim the lush Wallowa. Canyons give shelter against winter winds. Once deer and other game were plentiful, and the salmon came in such numbers that they formed living streams that ran uphill. As far as anyone can tell, Joseph's people took this home from no one. They came here long, long ago . . .

2

YOU WILL STAND HERE FOREVER
The World Chief Joseph Inherited

*L*ong, long ago, when the world was very young, seven giant brothers lived in the Blue Mountains. These giant monsters were taller than the tallest pines and stronger than the strongest oaks.

The ancient people feared these brothers greatly because they ate children. Each year the brothers traveled eastward and devoured all the little ones they could find. Mothers fled with their children and hid them, but still many were seized by the giants. The headmen in the villages feared that the tribe would soon be wiped out. But no one was big enough and strong enough to fight with seven giants at a time.

At last the headmen of the tribe decided to ask Coyote to help them. "Coyote is our friend," they said. "He has defeated other monsters. He will free us from the seven giants."

So they sent a messenger to Coyote. "Yes, I will help you," he promised. "I will free you from the seven giants."

But Coyote really did not know what to do. He had fought with giants. He had fought with monsters of the lakes and the rivers. But he knew he could not defeat seven giants at one time. So he asked his good friend Fox for advice.

"We will first dig seven holes," said his good friend Fox. "We will dig them very deep, in a place the giants always pass over when they travel to the east. Then we will fill the holes with boiling liquid."

So Coyote called together all the animals with claws—the beavers, the whistling marmots, the cougars, the bears and even the rats and mice and moles—to dig seven deep holes and carry water to them. His good friend Fox helped him keep the water boiling by dropping hot rocks into it.

11

Soon the time came for the giants' journey eastward. They marched along, all seven of them, their heads held high in the air. They were sure that no one dared to attack them. Coyote and Fox watched from behind some rocks and shrubs.

Down, down, down the seven giants went into the seven deep holes of boiling liquid. They struggled and struggled to get out, but the holes were very deep. They fumed and roared and splashed.

Then Coyote came out from his hiding place. The seven giants stood still. They knew Coyote.

"You are being punished for your wickedness," Coyote said to the seven giants. "I will punish you even more by changing you into seven mountains. I will make you very high, so that everyone can see you. You will stand here forever, to remind people that punishment comes from wrongdoing.

"And I will make a deep gash in the earth here, so that no more of your family can get across to trouble my people."

Coyote caused the seven giants to grow taller, and then he changed them into seven mountain peaks. He struck the earth a hard blow and so opened up a deep canyon at the feet of the giant peaks.

Today the mountain peaks are called the Seven Devils. The deep gorge at their feet is known as Hell's Canyon of the Snake River.

The stone giants described in this Nez Percé myth stand on the eastern side of North America's deepest gorge, Hell's Canyon. The Wallowa country, Joseph's home, lies to the west. For many miles in all directions lies one of the most varied and dramatic landscapes in the world: the plateau of the Pacific Northwest. The plateau stretches from the crest of the Rocky Mountains in present-day Montana and Yellowstone west to the Cascade Mountains in Oregon and Washington, from the dry plains of southern Idaho and Oregon north to the headwaters of the Columbia River in the Canadian Rockies. Cradled on all sides by mountains within the plateau lies the Columbia Plain, a hardened lava sea covering many thousand square miles in eastern Washington and central Idaho.

Two great river systems meet in the plain, the Columbia flowing from the north and the Snake from the south. The Snake River traces a long arc westward from the Yellowstone region across southern Idaho. Then it turns to the north and flows into Hell's Canyon. The Salmon and the Clearwater rivers twist west and north through the mountain country of today's central Idaho to join the Snake below Hell's Canyon. West of the canyon, the Imnaha, Wallowa and Grande Ronde rivers flow from the Wallowa and Blue mountains to the lower Snake.

The lower reaches of the Snake River and all these tributaries are networks of sheer-walled canyons and valleys etched deep into mountain and plain. Valleys lie just a few hundred feet above sea level, framed by 1,000- and 2,000-foot bluffs. In the spring of 1806, when Lewis and Clark camped on the green expanse of Weippe Prairie between the lower Clearwater River and mountains to the east, the mingling of alpine, high prairie and valley climates amazed them. "Within 20 miles of our camp we observe the rigors of winter cold, the cool air of spring, and the oppressive heat of midsummer," they wrote.

The ancestors of the Nez Percés and a number of related peoples reached the Columbia Plain perhaps 10,000 years ago, perhaps much earlier. Their ancestors in turn had worked their way slowly down the continent from the North, after the first people reached Alaska from Siberia thousands of years before. Here, in the Columbia Plain and the mountains around it, the people centered their lives on the salmon and the rivers that bore these bountiful and mysterious fish.

The fish, as an explorer later wrote, used to "swarm in myriads up the great rivers, and find their way up their main branches and into the minutest tributary streams, so as to pervade the great arid plains and to penetrate even among barren mountains." The salmon seek the cold, oxygen-rich waters of mountain streams to lay their eggs. Hatching in spring, their young once rode down swollen streams and rivers for hundreds of miles, changing from fresh to saltwater fish and heading out to sea. The grown fish returned in their millions to the rivers. Some species came in spring and some in summer or fall.

The Nez Percés settled up the Snake River and into Hell's Canyon and by the Clearwater, Salmon, Grande Ronde and Imnaha rivers and their tributaries. Besides fishing the rivers, the people found edible roots in the high prairies and berries and game in the hills and mountains. But they were mainly a river dwelling people. Rivers carried their major source of food and—in the lower sections—their canoes. Archaeologists have found two dwelling sites in the lower Clearwater Valley that are about 10,000 years old. They found an 8,000-year-old "buffalo jump"—a place where the animals were stampeded over a cliff—near the Snake River in the southeastern corner of Washington. It was a fairly easy trip by canoe from those early camps. But at some point the buffalo disappeared from the Columbia Plain.

Originally, Joseph's own Nez Percé band lived mostly in a small portion of the Wallowa country, the canyon of the lower Grande Ronde River. They followed salmon runs up the Grande Ronde's side canyons, especially the well-sheltered creek bottoms that led south. Occasionally some people from the band hunted still farther south, in the rolling forest and pasture land around the Wallowa River. Near this river's source they found a deep, pristine lake teeming with salmon and other fish.

Nez Percé communities varied in size from perhaps 200 people at rich fishing grounds in lower valleys to a dozen or so on remote mountain streams. The people of a village lived together as extended families, held the food supply in common and harvested fish, game and plants cooperatively. Their homes were rectangular wood-frame lodges covered with mats of woven reeds—the larger the village, the longer its main dwelling.

People worked spring, summer and fall to build up reserves of food against the winter starving time. They dried fish, meat, berries and roots or roasted loaves of mashed roots. They passed winter in their long houses, telling tales and making tools and weapons of stone, bone, horn, sinew and wood. They wove bags and watertight baskets from plant stems and made dugout canoes from tree trunks.

They called themselves the People. When the first European-Americans reached the region in the late 1700s, French traders got the idea that most of them wore ornaments in their noses and so misnamed them "Pierced Noses," or Nez Percés. English traders called them Green Wood Indians for awhile, but it was the French name that stuck.

After thousands of years, this stable culture began to change rapidly in response to a totally new and unfamiliar creature: the horse. As the Spanish built settlements a thousand miles away along the Rio Grande in present day New Mexico during the 1600s, they brought horses with them. Some animals escaped and some were stolen by southwestern tribes. Through trading and raiding between tribes, the horse spread across the deserts and mountains of the Southwest, until the People obtained their first mounts not long after 1700. In the decades that followed, their herds grew rapidly. No group had so much pasture and such strong natural defenses. The Nez Percés may have been the only tribe in North America to learn selective breeding. They moved rapidly from a life of constant food gathering to the creation of wealth—horses—which both aided the quest for food directly and was traded for food and many other useful things.

Horses allowed the people of the lower Grande Ronde River to range freely across the Wallowa country. The people fattened their animals in the luxuriant pastures around the Wallowa River and took good advantage of fishing, hunting and plant foods. The canyons of the Grande Ronde and its lower tributaries remained the best wintering grounds; the Imnaha River Valley, in the remote eastern part of the Wallowa country also offered good winter pasture. The Imnaha, flowing north to the Snake, has cut a deep swathe through rugged mountains. The towering ridges on either side deflect winter storms, while from the south the sun reaches between the ridges to the valley floor.

The beauty, seclusion and plenty of the Wallowa country made it special to its inhabitants. Wallowa Lake, where eagles glided above the surrounding mountains, was a favorite campground and a sacred place.

The horse also brought closer relations among different bands of the tribe. The huge increase in the range of hunting and food gathering required more widespread cooperation. Bands joined together for protection against mounted raiders who were enticed by the large supply of horses. The horse brought more contact with neighboring tribes, such as the Cayuses, Wallawallas, Palouses and Yakimas, who lived to the west. They and the Nez Percés were part of a family of peoples, sometimes called the Sahaptins, who spoke related languages and often intermarried.

To the east, the Nez Percés developed close relations with an unrelated group, the Salish of the Bitterroot Valley in western Montana. These people, who had also become a mounted society, hunted buffalo in the broad valleys scattered among the Rockies and in the Great Plains to the east. They often traded buffalo products to the Nez Percés or traveled and hunted with them. In the mountainous country between their homelands (around the present-day boundary between northern Idaho and Montana) Nez Percés and Salish lived together and intermarried, just as the Nez Percés mingled with their relations and neighbors to the west. The Nez Percés also traded and usually got along with other Salish groups who lived on the Columbia Plain and in the mountains of northern Idaho. A variety of relations developed with tribes to the south and with those of the Great Plains, ranging from mixtures of trade and conflict to traditions of rivalry and war. The Nez Percés were fierce fighters who eagerly avenged attacks on their homes or hunting and trading parties.

But above all they enjoyed the mobility and the wealth created by their unique relationship with the horse. Before the coming of the horse they had traded downriver by canoe as far west as the Cascades, where they got shells and dried seafood from coastal peoples. With the horse the Nez Percés reached east through the mountains and deep into the plains, where they hunted and traded for buffalo products. They exchanged horses, ram-horn bows, dried fish, fish oil and goods from the coast for buffalo robes and meat, tools of buffalo horn and bone, and other goods they could not find at home.

Of all the western tribes, none surpassed the outreach of the Nez Percés or their ability to borrow from the cultures they encountered. They spoke the Chinook trade language of the Pacific coast and communicated with peoples of the mountains and the Great Plains with sign language. They adopted practical things like the tipi but also dance steps, religious customs, headdresses and other showy attire of the plains peoples.

The tipi—a tall, cone-shaped frame of poles covered with hide—provided a roomy shelter for one or two families and was easily taken down and moved. The same poles and hides were used as travois, with which horses could haul baggage or people. The Nez Percés also learned to stretch buffalo hides over round frames of wood to make bullboats, small craft that horses towed across rivers with loads of people and baggage. Thanks to these innovations an entire community could travel great distances—men, women and children, old and young, sick people as well as healthy ones.

The only practical route to or from the East for bands hauling baggage on travois lay along the Clark Fork River, which flows northeast out of the Rockies in Montana to join the Columbia in Canada. Its gently sloping valley provided an easy passage between the north end of the Bitterroot Valley and the northwest side of the Columbia Plain. Lightly burdened groups, usually men traveling without families, could use more direct routes to the Bitterroot that were too rugged for the travois. These, including the Lolo Trail that Lewis and Clark followed in 1805 and 1806, ran along steep mountain ridges through the Clearwater and Salmon river countries.

As they traveled west down the Snake and Columbia and east through the mountains in the late 1700s, the Nez Percés began to find new and fascinating items in the hands of their trading partners. Ships from Europe, mostly from Britain, began calling along the Northwest coast to exchange manufactured goods for furs. French and British traders brought their goods across Canada by canoe along a network of lakes and rivers. Before they saw any white men the Nez Percés had heard of them and obtained colorful woolen blankets, metal

A Nez Percé child in a cradleboard, circa 1900
(Courtesy Historical Photograph Collections, Washington State University)

arrowheads, knives, pots, utensils and beads. These items saved labor and encouraged more elaborate crafts. Nez Percé women did intricate bead work on moccasins, clothing, and on the bags they made from plant stems. These articles too were soon in demand at trading centers.

But toward the end of the 1700s the new flow of trade carried two more things into the Northwest that threatened entire tribes with chaos and death: the gun and the diseases of the white European- Americans. The natives had no natural resistance to the smallpox, measles, influenza, typhus, cholera, scarlet fever and other diseases that entered the trade stream. Some coastal tribes were virtually wiped out. Starting before 1800, diseases moved up the Columbia and Snake and struck the Nez Percés repeatedly. Many died, and the number of children surviving to maturity dropped. The People were shaken and looked for new sources of guidance and spiritual power in the struggle to survive.

As disease reduced populations, firearms introduced from the East trapped native peoples in a cycle of violence, dependence and migration. Guns tipped the scales drastically in relations between tribes, giving an overwhelming advantage in both hunting and war to groups that possessed them over groups that did not. To get guns and steady supplies of ammunition most people had no choice but to begin trapping fur-bearing animals. The traders demanded furs for their merchandise because furs brought good cash prices in the markets of Europe.

The fur trade penetrated North America most rapidly through Hudson Bay, the Great Lakes and along river systems stretching far into what is today the Canadian west. The woodlands around these waterways were rich in furs. The broad Missouri River in the United States also led to good trapping grounds in the eastern Rockies. But the British, unlike the Americans to the south, had plenty of cash to invest in the lucrative trade.

Thousands of Native Americans moved away from hunting and gathering and into dependence on a market economy based in Europe and dominated by Europeans. As they cleaned out the fur bearing animals in their own areas, native groups turned west to new trapping grounds. With their guns they drove away groups who had only bows and arrows. These displaced groups in turn pressured others farther west, and they all faced an uncertain future if they could not obtain firearms. Conflict and war were certainly no strangers to the world of Native Americans. But the fur trade destroyed the order of their world and increased the frequency and destructiveness of violence.

The Nez Percés and other peoples in the western mountains first faced this threat at the hands of the Blackfeet and allied tribes who lived on the western reaches of the river trading routes, on both sides of today's boundary between Canada and the United States. After the mid-1700s, when the Blackfeet obtained their first guns, they became increasingly warlike and hungry for horses. They drove some Salish groups west into northern Idaho and raided deep into the territory of the Nez Percés and tribes to the south. The Clarks Fork River trade route became a death trap. The Blackfeet attacked Nez Percé hunters in the Great Plains and did all they could to block trade and keep the mountain tribes from obtaining guns. The ships that traded on the Northwest coast brought a variety of goods, but no firearms.

In 1805, when Lewis and Clark reached the Nez Percés, a group of their daring men had just managed to evade the Blackfeet and brought back a few guns from friendlier groups farther east. Over the next two decades British traders moved across the Great Divide in Canada to the Columbia River and down the Columbia to the sea. Officially, they had agreed to share the territory of the Northwest with the Americans. But, with their system for distributing goods and collecting furs over a vast expanse of the continent, the British overwhelmed their competitors. They took over Fort Astoria, an American trading post near the mouth of the Columbia, in 1812. Six years later they built Fort Nez Percés on the Columbia at the mouth of the Walla Walla River, just downstream from the mouth of the Snake River. The post was later renamed Fort Walla Walla. In 1825, as Britain's Hudson's Bay Company tightened its hold on the region, it established a major post on the lower Columbia River, Fort Vancouver, with its own farm, shops and mills. Next year a similar post, Fort Colville, opened farther upriver on the north side of the Columbia Plain.

Yet the British, like the Americans who continued probing the region, found they could not dictate the rules of the fur trade in the Northwest as they had to native peoples east of the Rocky Mountains. The canoe might carry people and goods up and down the broad waterways of the Columbia Plain with ease, but it was worthless in the treacherous gorges and steep riverbeds elsewhere in the mountainous Northwest interior. British and American traders had to look to native people for the only practical means of transportation, the horse, and organize their own expeditions to do the trapping. British expeditions moved south from Fort Walla Walla to reach the rich trapping grounds of the upper Snake River basin. The route ran southeast through the Blue Mountains to the broad valley of the upper Grande Ronde River and continued in the same direction, skirting the Wallowa Mountains, to reach the Snake River Plain.

Thus the horseback peoples, particularly the Nez Percés, were able to obtain guns, ammunition and other goods without becoming trappers. Thanks to the horse, they dealt with whites as equals, using a sustainable source of wealth instead of a source, like furs, that could be wiped out. A horse was the property of an individual among Native Americans much as it was among whites. Horse rearing, training and trading fostered individual and family enterprise. But horses did not uproot the old river dwelling culture. Rather, they gave new meaning to the old group values. Cooperation was essential to manage and protect the herds and to travel in faraway and sometimes dangerous places. The mobility provided by horses also allowed bands to return to the rivers regularly for fish harvests and winter shelter, and there they continued the old ways of life alongside the new.

They moved back into long houses or used their tipi poles and hides to form long "compound" tipis that were similar to the older communal dwellings. These group homes reemerged whenever bands gathered to fish at the rivers or dig roots from the prairies, to race horses, to hold festivals and councils. And within them the People continued to affirm kinship as the basis for self-government and the root of life, and to tell the stories that explained it all to their children.

Here, as a child, Joseph heard the myth of the Seven Devils, one among hundreds of tales that described creation as a web of kinship embracing people, plants, animals and the earth. Myths recounted the making of mountains and mosquitos, such details as the markings of the raccoon, and bigger questions, like the creation of humans and the existence of death, which every human must some day face. The myths taught that people and earth were part of the same creation.

Some stories, like the myth of the Seven Devils, were tales with a moral. In this legend the animal kingdom responds to the summons of Coyote to intervene in a crisis and protect the People. This act traps the monsters and unleashes Coyote's mystical power. The myth taught Joseph that children are precious, that exploitation of the weak by the powerful is wrong and that cooperation among humble beings can defeat a seemingly invincible evil.

3

CHILD OF THE NEZ PERCÉS
1834–54

From the moment of his birth Joseph lived at the center of his community, in the home of its chief, his father. Throughout his childhood and youth he witnessed his people's daily process of self-government. He was his father's student from an early age, and the council that deliberated around his father's fire was his school.

In any Nez Percé village, issues great and small were settled around the camp fire of the chief, in front of everyone. Here it was the duty of the adult men to decide how to feed their families and keep them safe. This was the place to plan hunts and resolve disputes, to bring news and to hear it. Harry Wheeler, a Nez Percé who lived near the Clearwater River, explained it to a scholar, Haruo Aoki, in 1960.

> In the evening people used to gather at a chief's house and smoke a pipe while they deliberated and talked about taking trips, hunting, fishing and anything else. If they observed anything, buffalos or people, the Bannocks, the Blackfoot, the Sioux [tribes that sometimes fought the Nez Percés], or anything, they brought in the news and over the smoke men talked. They made plans, as "What is best to do?" They discussed the country where they would be going, or where the buffalos were moving. They did not just smoke (for nothing) but they deliberated on everything. . . . Indians learned the news over the smoke, before hunting, before making a journey, sorrow, or before anything. By that, they made plans, and that was what smoking the pipe was. Starting with the chief, they passed the pipe around. . . .
>
> Their first thought was about a journey for camping. The journey was hazardous. It was hazardous possibly because

of cold weather, or possibly because of rain. They used to run ahead to see the campsite—if it was good for horses, if the place was good for staying, had enough good wood, and also good water, . . .
 If there were any troubles, they would discuss that matter first. Because no one would take trips with worries, they tried to resolve them to full satisfaction. For this reason the camp was free from worries and they were peaceful where they camped.

Joseph's father, Tuekakas, was head chief of the Wallowa band. He was the son of a Wallowa woman and a man from a Cayuse band that lived in the hills and table lands between the Blue Mountains and the Columbia River. Before Tuekakas's birth in the late 1780s, his mother left his father and returned to her own people. Tuekakas grew up among the Nez Percés. As a young man he lived for a time with his Cayuse family but then returned to the Wallowa country. There Khap-khap-onmi, the daughter of a Wallowa chief, married him. When her father grew old the people made Tuekakas their leader.

Tuekakas married other women as well. Men took greater risks in hunting, travel to far off places and in war, so women outnumbered them. Successful hunters and horse breeders, who could support larger families, often lived with more than one wife. Men took the lead in decision making within a band, but a man did not have the power to make decisions for his wife. Women owned the tipis, the food supplies, household goods and some of the horses. If a woman left her husband, she took her children and belongings. If she remarried, her children became the shared responsibility of the new husband.

Joseph was born to Khap-khap-onmi probably in early 1840 when his people were in the canyons of the northern Wallowa country. Legend has it that his birthplace was a cave by Joseph Creek, a stream flowing north through a broad wooded canyon to the lower Grande Ronde.

No one kept records of the complex family relations among the Nez Percés. Until they met white people they had never heard of the written word. We know only that, because of plural marriage and intermarriage between bands and tribes, Joseph had an assortment of relatives in his home, within the Wallowa band and among the Nez Percés and Cayuse peoples. He had at least four full or half brothers and sisters: a sister known today only by a name whites later gave her, Celia; Elawinonmi, another sister; and two full brothers, Shugun and Ollokot. The youngest, Ollokot, was born in the early 1840s.

Like any Nez Percé child, Joseph traveled about on horseback from birth, bound up in a cradleboard on his mother's back, and as soon as he was large enough, tied into a wood-frame saddle. As a toddler he spent a lot of time with elders, who told him tales and taught him crafts. "It was our custom for the old people to instruct the children," Yellow Wolf, a nephew of Joseph's who grew up in the Wallowa, recalled in later years. They learned how to make bows and arrows, shoot at targets and hunt small game. They learned crafts and the harvesting and storage of food. Their accomplishments were praised and celebrated. Garments, tools and toys were carefully made and given throughout the extended family as signs of affection.

The clearest account of the democracy that Joseph learned about under his father's leadership dates from several years before his birth. In February of 1834 Benjamin E. Bonneville, a captain in the U.S. Army who had taken leave to explore the uncharted Northwest, staggered into the Imnaha Valley with a small group of men and horses. He later told his story to a popular author of the day, Washington Irving, who wrote a book about it.

Bonneville left Missouri in 1832 and crossed the Great Plains and the Rocky Mountains (which were not yet part of the United States). He spent some of that year and the next with the Salmon River Nez Percés. Early in 1834 Bonneville set out to inspect the British trading posts of the Columbia River and with his men blundered into Hell's Canyon from the north. They eventually climbed out of the canyon and moved west through a bleak and windswept landscape until, weak and starving, they reached the green floor of the Imnaha Valley. There two small groups of Nez Percés gave them food and guided them toward the lower Grande Ronde and the main winter camp of the Wallowa people. The leader of one group sent a runner ahead to tell Tuekakas he had a guest from the people of Lewis and Clark.

As Bonneville and his men passed a hill near the Grande Ronde, Irving wrote, "the whole population of the village broke upon their view, drawn out in the most imposing style, and arrayed in all their finery. The effect of the whole was wild and fantastic yet singularly striking. In the front rank were the chiefs and principal warriors, glaringly painted and decorated. Behind them were arranged the rest of the people, men, women and children." The white men dismounted and all the people, starting with the chiefs, came forward to shake hands. Irving reported that

> Mats, poles and other materials were now brought and a comfortable lodge was soon erected for the strangers, where they were kept constantly supplied with wood and water and other necessaries; and all their effects were placed in safekeeping. Their horses, too, were unsaddled, and turned loose to graze and a guard set to keep watch upon them.
>
> All this being adjusted they were conducted to the main building or council house of the village, where an ample repast, or rather banquet was spread, which seemed to realize all the gastronomical dreams that had tantalized them during their long starvation; for here they beheld not merely fish and roots in abundance, but the flesh of deer and elk, and the choicest pieces of buffalo meat.

When his guests had eaten their fill Tuekakas presided over a long dialog between his people and the visitors.

> The chief showed the same curiosity evinced by his tribe generally to obtain information concerning the United States . . . as their traffic is almost exclusively with the British traders. Captain Bonneville did his best to set forth the merits of his nation, and the importance of their friendship to the red men . . . The chief and all present listened with profound attention, and evidently with great interest; nor were the important facts thus set forth confined to the audience in the lodge; for sentence after sentence was loudly repeated by a crier for the benefit of the whole village.
>
> A village has generally several of these walking newspapers, as they are termed by the whites, who go about proclaiming the news of the day, giving notice of public councils, expeditions, dances, feasts and other ceremonials, and advertizing anything lost. While Captain Bonne-

ville remained among the Nez Percés, if a glove, handkerchief or anything of similar value, was lost or mislaid, it was carried by the finder to the lodge of the chief, and proclamation was made by one of their criers, for the owner to come and claim his property.

The sharing of information throughout the band went along with shared authority. The year after Bonneville's visit Samuel Parker, a clergyman who visited the Nez Percés, observed that chiefs "do not exercise authority by command but use their influence by persuasion" to bring about consensus. "Probably there is no government on earth where there is so much personal and political freedom and at the same time so little anarchy," he wrote. ". . . The day may be rued [regretted] when their order and harmony shall be interrupted."

But, as Bonneville had noticed, that order and harmony was already under strain. He saw some nearly destitute Nez Percé bands along the upper Salmon River. The Blackfeet raided into this area so often in 1833 that these people lost most of their horses. Conflict had worn these Idaho Nez Percés down. Instead of going after the Blackfeet, they traveled to relatives on the other side of the Snake River, who were less exposed to attack, and who gave them horses.

Though the Wallowa people were more secure and more prosperous, disease and mounted, gun-toting enemies had darkened their world too. Near the Grande Ronde River Bonneville saw the grave of a Wallowa man raiders had killed. By the 1830s the population of the Nez Percés had fallen sharply because of disease. There were probably fewer than 3,000 of them, compared to 6,000 or more a quarter century before. Tuekakas had seen all this in his lifetime. He had seen the coming of the British and of the Americans. Bonneville told his Nez Percé friends that the Americans "were as countless as the blades of grass in the prairies, and that, great as Snake River was, if they were all encamped upon its banks they would drink it dry in a single day . . ."

The world was changing. There was more to discuss around the council fire than hunting, fishing and travel. Like other chiefs, Tuekakas had a duty to seek a path for his people. He became one of the most active leaders of his tribe in this search.

Just as the People had adopted headdresses, dance steps, cures, languages and more from other tribes, they learned all they could about the white people and borrowed anything they thought might be of benefit. They were especially interested in finding out how the whites got their amazing powers to create weapons and tools of metal and to cure disease. Many Nez Percés picked up a smattering of Christianity from white traders and from a Nez Percé boy who attended a British school in Canada. They heard about a book, the Bible, given to the white people by God. It must have seemed like something similar to the songs and instructions spirits gave to Nez Percés in visions and dreams.

Some of the hard pressed Nez Percés of what is now Idaho took special interest in the Americans, who traveled into the Rocky Mountains to trap and trade. They too were enemies of the Blackfeet, unlike the British who supplied the Blackfeet with guns. The Americans were easygoing and friendly, unlike the British, and less stingy in trade. The Americans had sent Lewis and Clark, who had promised the Nez Percés that the Great Father who ruled in the East would bring them peace and trade.

Protestants in the United States heard during the early 1830s that the Nez Percés were asking the Americans for teachers. Many of the faithful believed they were under a sacred obligation, direct from God, to save the souls of "heathens" all over the world before the Second Coming of Christ, when the unsaved would be cast into hellfire. Protestants were also goaded by the idea that the Indians might be left to the Catholic missionaries who followed the British into the Northwest. A clamor rose for the American Board of Foreign Missions, a group set up by the larger Protestant denominations, to send missionaries into the wilderness to "save the savages."

The Pacific Northwest lay beyond the boundaries of the United States and at this time was claimed by both the U.S. and Britain. Unwittingly, the Nez Percés were caught up in the contest between the two powers over who would get this land. It held fortunes in fur and timber, and the potential for ports that could tap the rich markets of Asia. By the 1830s the British had taken control of the territory north of the Columbia River. To the south, they tried to strip the entire Snake River region of furs, hoping to discourage the Americans who ventured there and so keep them from spreading north.

The British succeeded in holding American fur traders back. But they did not foresee that American missionaries who came to convert Indians would soon bring in thousands of American settlers after them. Henry and Eliza Spalding, the missionary couple who in 1836 moved to Nez Percé country on the lower Clearwater River, were in fact settlers themselves.

Spalding was a slender, intense man who looked to his mission for the economic security, status and happiness he never knew among whites. He was born in 1803. His parents abandoned him in infancy, and he spent his childhood living with a farming family in the isolated hills of western New York state, working long hours for his food and receiving no education. In 1820 his foster father drove him from home with a whip.

Spalding managed to live as a farm laborer and began to attend school. He joined the Congregational church in Prattsburg, New York, and with its help completed his basic education. For a while he scratched a meager living as a teacher, and then he decided to study for the ministry. He joined the Presbyterians, a denomination that conceived of ministers as leaders of their communities, with responsibility for the personal, temporal and spiritual lives of their flocks. Rather than wait for a job ministering to the converted in an established congregation, Spalding chose a quicker path to leadership and one he considered far more important: conversion of the "heathen."

Spalding's fervor for saving souls did not lead him to believe in their equal worth. While he was studying for the ministry at Lane Theological Seminary near Cincinnati in 1834, the student movement against slavery caused an upheaval. Of 44 students, 40 left in protest when the seminary suppressed the student abolition society. Spalding was one of the four who stayed.

That year he and Eliza Hart married. Raised in a farming family near Prattsburg, she shared Spalding's religion, his views and his belief in missionary work, though she was more patient and tolerant than he. In 1836 missionary Marcus Whitman recruited the Spaldings to join him and his wife Narcissa in founding a mission in the Pacific Northwest. The American Board of Foreign Missions provided money for food and supplies. The two couples joined a brigade of fur trappers and made the difficult journey across the Great Plains and the Rocky Mountains to the Snake River Plain in what is now southern Idaho. Crossing the plain, they picked up the British trappers' route, leaving the river above Hell's Canyon, and traveling northwest through the Grande Ronde Valley and the Blue Mountains to the Columbia River.

Bands of Cayuse and Clearwater Nez Percés, who were anxious to learn the powers of white people, urged the missionaries to settle with them. Henry Spalding did not get along well with the Whitmans anyway, so the two couples decided to set up separate mission stations. The Whitmans settled with the Cayuse between the Blue Mountains and the Columbia, at a place called Waiilatpu upstream from the British fort on the Walla Walla River. Their mission site lies in what is today southeastern Washington state, near the town of Walla Walla. The Nez Percés persuaded the Spaldings to settle about 200 miles away, in present-day Idaho, near the lower Clearwater River on Lapwaii Creek.

Spalding's feelings of superiority and his plans to make the Nez Percés into carbon copies of white Presbyterian farmers were not immediately clear to the People. He thought of himself as one of "God's people" who chose "abode for life among the polluted heathen." After he reached Lapwaii he declared that "the Lord appointed me my work in this portion of his vineyard . . ." and his task was to "root up the thorns and break up the fallow ground"—that is, to uproot the "heathen" Nez Percé culture.

Several other whites soon joined the Spaldings, and with the help of many Nez Percés they went to work at Lapwaii building houses, workshops, mills, a school and a church, plowing land, fencing fields, planting grain, potatoes and fruit trees and raising cattle and sheep. Spalding gave the Nez Percés trade goods and farm implements in exchange for their labor. He taught some of them how to raise wheat and other crops and helped with their harvest, taking a portion of it as payment. Another missionary started a mission station farther up the Clearwater, at Kamiah.

Spalding viewed his station at Lapwaii as the property of his church. It did not belong to the Nez Percés; the Nez Percés belonged to it. When the American Board of Foreign Missions considered abandoning its struggling missions in the North-

One of the first buildings erected by the Spaldings for living and teaching quarters on the Clearwater River at Lapwaii Creek. (Courtesy Historical Photograph Collections, Washington State University)

west, Spalding pleaded with the board "to retain this station and what pertains to it, viz, the mills, shops, printing establishment, cattle, horses and sheep, and the Nez Percés people." Eliza wrote her parents about their orchards and fields of corn and wheat. "The labor on the farm," she added, "is mostly performed by natives."

Spalding had trouble with the Nez Percé language in his efforts to teach church doctrine to the natives. He used what he could learn, drawings and at times the aid of a Nez Percé who knew some English. In a diary he wrote of speaking at meetings of "the law of God, its glorious tendencies, all tending to good, to life, the basis of the universe." From birth, he preached, all people were tainted by sin. "We are all lost, ruined creatures by our act of sin and there is no life for us in ourselves or in creation." Only by accepting Christ through the church and becoming one of the people of God, like Spalding, could any wretched soul find hope for redemption. Acceptance of Christ meant submission to the government of the church, and in particular to Spalding, who considered it proper to whip native people for such offenses as gambling or leaving an abusive husband.

Tuekakas was one of the first two Nez Percés whom Spalding decided had embraced his doctrine enough to merit membership in the church. He baptized the chief in 1839, naming him Joseph. Later whites would call Tuekakas Old Joseph to distinguish him from his son Joseph. "The law of God was brought plain to his mind" Spalding wrote of his new convert, and "penetrated his heart like an arrow . . . He is anxious to unite with the people of God and work for Him the remainder of his life. His soul is in agony for his people."

Just how much of this was true is hard to say. One of the other missionaries bluntly accused Spalding of wishful thinking. Tuekakas no doubt made a determined effort to learn all he could from Spalding and apply it to his own situation. It seems clear he was indeed deeply concerned for the future of his people. But it seems unlikely that he had any intention of abandoning the spiritual beliefs and way of life of his own culture. Some of the Nez Percés who clustered around Spalding decided to follow him, to adopt the ways of whites and turn away from their own heritage. Some opposed Spalding and became openly hostile to him. Tuekakas steered a middle course.

He and some of his people came to stay at Lapwaii often. They worked for Spalding and attended Eliza's school. Tuekakas learned to read in his own language, and for more than a decade he kept a portion of the New Testament that the missionaries translated into the Nez Percé language and printed at Lapwaii. Tuekakas dabbled in farming at Lapwaii and learned about cattle there. He quickly realized these animals presented the opportunity for a new food source. He later acquired some and began raising them in the Wallowa country.

But Tuekakas did not settle at Lapwaii or take up serious farming, as some other Nez Percés did. One of Tuekakas's wives also joined Spalding's church, and they had children baptized. Other Wallowa people did not join, nor did they take up farming. Yet Tuekakas continued as their chief. He pursued his duty as a leader to learn useful things from the powerful white people and to learn how they thought and how to deal with them. If the whites believed in a divine law and lived by it, as Spalding claimed, surely it would be wise to understand this law.

On a spring day in 1840, Spalding took the infant son of Tuekakas and Khap-khap-onmi in his hands for baptism. He gave the child a Christian name, Ephraim, which never stuck. As a toddler, Joseph said, he spent some time in Eliza's school. He left the school by the age of five or six. At some time in his life, perhaps as early as this, Joseph learned to view schools as agents of indoctrination. Other than this, there is no evidence that the Spaldings made much of an impression of him.

The year of Joseph's birth was a momentous one for the Northwest and for the onset of the conflict that would consume Joseph's life. The fur trade collapsed completely because Europeans stopped buying furs and the territory had been stripped of the supply.

With the fur trade gone, some of the mountain men—as the trappers and traders living in the wilderness were known—headed for the lush Willamette Valley, near Fort Vancouver. One group started in southern Idaho and for the first time brought wagons from the Snake River Plain through the Blue Mountains to the Columbia River. They opened the Oregon Trail, and word of it soon spread to the East. Encouraged by the federal government, settlers began trickling in to homestead in the Willamette. In 1842 the government appointed an agent for Indian affairs in the Northwest, Elijah White, and subsidized an expedition that brought White and 100 settlers across the Great Plains, through the Rockies to the Oregon Trail.

The next year Whitman, who had returned briefly to the eastern United States, led 1,000 people down the Oregon Trail. "The majority of them are farmers lured by the prospect of bounty in lands, by the reported fertility of the soil and by the desire to be first among those who are planting our institutions on the Pacific coast," the missionary wrote in a letter to the U.S. War Department. He gave details of the route and suggested points along the way where posts should be set up to keep Native Americans in line and to sell provisions for the "immense migration of families" that would be heading for the Willamette.

Whitman did all he could to foster the migration. He had not done very well with conversion of "heathens" to farming at Waiilatpu. But now his station became a resting spot for the white travelers. Spalding lost no time in exploiting this ready market for horses and produce brought from Lapwaii. He even rode back down the trail to meet the settlers with his goods.

Relations soon became less pleasant between missionaries and natives at both Waiilatpu and Lapwaii. The white people were streaming through the land of the Cayuse, and the link between the migrants and the missionaries was plain enough. Native people wondered where it would lead. Spalding and Whitman began to fear for their own safety.

In 1843 Elijah White, the Indian agent, came to Lapwaii and met with Tuekakas and about 20 other chiefs. He told them he had been sent by the Great Father in the East to gain their agreement to the same laws that white people lived by. He assured them that if they submitted to the law it would protect them and their people too. The chiefs agreed to a code covering crimes, from trespassing to murder. Penalties ranged from fines to whipping and hanging. White agreed that the chiefs should have authority to punish offenses committed by Nez Percés and took responsibility on himself for punishing whites who committed crimes against Nez Percés. The chiefs agreed to have Ellis, a younger Nez Percés man who could read and write English, act as head chief in dealings with the whites on legal matters. But the chiefs could not have understood this as empowering Ellis to speak for the whole tribe on any subject. White made similar agreements with other tribes. But when whites began to commit crimes against Native Americans, he did nothing.

The white immigration swelled to a flood, bringing 3,000 people along the Oregon Trail in 1845. New diseases began to ravage the Cayuse population around Waiilatpu, and these people grew increasingly desperate and suspicious of Whitman. Some of Spalding's followers among the Nez Percés remained committed to the path of farming and Presbyterianism, but his buildings were repeatedly vandalized, his mills and irrigation works damaged. The school closed in 1846.

Tuekakas and others from the Wallowa country had by this time stopped staying at the mission. What he thought of all these events was never recorded. But, with the Oregon Trail passing to the south of the Wallowa Mountains, he could not have failed to notice these things. He and his people may well have traded horses for cattle with the settlers as they came through the Grande Ronde Valley.

In 1847 some of the Cayuse leaders concluded that Whitman was responsible for the disease that was decimating their population and that he intended to destroy the tribe and give its land to the settlers. With guns and tomahawks, they massacred the Whitmans and some of their helpers at Waiilatpu. Spalding, who was in the area at the time, barely escaped and made it back to Lapwaii. He soon fled with his family to the Willamette.

The Willamette settlers regarded Whitman as a saint for bringing the first large wagon train down the Oregon Trail. Some of them had fought Native Americans in the East and learned to hate them. In 1848 they sent an army of more than 400 men east into the country of the Cayuse who, after two days of inconclusive fighting, gave way and dispersed. A Cayuse brother of Tuekakas, wounded in the battle, fled to the Wallowa country and was taken in. Tuekakas and the other Nez Percé chiefs managed to keep their people at peace as the settler army stormed around the country of the lower Snake River, from Waiilatpu and Fort Walla to the Clearwater and on to Lapwaii, in a fruitless search for the Whitmans' murderers. The frustrated volunteers engaged in random killing and livestock stealing among other tribes and at one point were attacked and driven back to Waiilatpu by warriors of the Palouse people, who lived along the lower Snake. Before heading home the whites announced that the lands of the Cayuse in the Walla Walla Valley had been forfeited to the whites.

Then the Americans, the soldiers and the last of the missionaries, left. For the next seven years after the Cayuse War they found more profitable things to do near the coast, and the Nez Percés had their country to themselves.

But in those years the United States closed in on them by leaps and bounds. When Joseph was a child in the Wallowa country during the later 1840s and early 1850s, the United States acquired vast territories in the west and began the destruction of Native American groups between the Pacific Ocean and the Rocky Mountains. In 1846 the United States and Britain settled their dispute over the Pacific Northwest.

President James Polk negotiated the Oregon Treaty with Britain, dividing the territory in two along the present U.S.-Canadian boundary. The United States gained present-day Oregon, Washington, Idaho and parts of Montana and Wyoming. Just two years later, as a result of war with Mexico, the United States acquired California and the rest of the Southwest, from the Rio Grande and the Gila River all the way to the Pacific Northwest.

These acquisitions brought a vast empire into American possession. And in 1849 something far more alluring than furs—gold—set a worldwide stampede in motion to occupy and exploit this empire. The frenzied rush to California drew migration away from the Northwest for a few years. In global terms it caused a dramatic shift in population to the Pacific coast of North America and the near-total destruction of the native peoples living there. As California filled up and mines were stripped, the invading whites would probe hungrily into the surrounding regions, seeking new sources of wealth.

None of this could have been apparent to a Nez Percé boy growing up within the seclusion of the Wallowa country, herding his father's livestock, learning to breed it, learning to use firearms and joining hunts in the mountains. Joseph certainly saw the covered wagons moving through the Grande Ronde Valley. He saw his wounded Cayuse uncle and heard of the Cayuse War and other news of the Americans at his father's fire. But life got better for his own people. Their growing herds of beef ended the need for long and dangerous trips to the buffalo country. The need of white settlers for horses replaced the market lost with the end of the fur trade. The Wallowa Nez Percés continued to change and live in their own way, holding fast to their own form of government and beliefs.

As a boy of 12 or so Joseph began to cross from childhood to maturity in the traditional way, by means of personal contact with the spirits who lived in a world of shadows alongside the tangible world of the living. He had learned something of this as a child through the myths he heard and at festivals where adults danced and sang in mysterious reenactments of their encounters with spirits. He also learned to interpret his dreams as visits from supernatural beings.

The spirits were the natural forces, plants, animals and cycles of life on the earth. They would share their powers with people who learned how to reach into their world and follow their instructions. A spirit could sustain a desperate hunter, though far from home and weak for lack of food; it could give guidance to someone who was lost, give power in battle or the power to drive away evil spirits that caused illness. Native Americans viewed spirits as essential allies in the struggle for survival. This is why they at first believed that the firearms, medical skills and the other amazing powers white people had must signify great wisdom and spiritual strength.

Among the Nez Percés, as among most Native Americans, it was almost unheard of for anyone to talk openly about the spiritual encounters that were a traditional rite of passage for youth. Joseph, when questioned as an old man, referred to his

Tuekakas, or Old Joseph (c. 1785–1870), was leader of the Wallowa band of Nez Percés before his son, Joseph. This portrait was done in 1855. (Courtesy Washington State Historical Society, Tacoma, Washington)

own experience very briefly. But Yellow Wolf gave some details of how he got his spirit power to a close white friend who wrote the story down. Yellow Wolf's story has some bearing on Joseph's.

"Beginning with the forefathers of all Indians," he explained, "they had such a power given to them—different spirits coming out of once living animals. Also from the thunder, the wind, the sun, the earth, rocks, or whatever it might be. This power descends from one person to another . . . It came to me from my father."

His parents sent him out, he said, one spring when he was about 13, "gave me one blanket, but no food. I might go 15, maybe 20 suns with nothing to eat, but could drink water aplenty. Only trees for shelter, and fir brush to sleep on. I might stay in one place three nights, maybe five nights, then go somewhere else. Nobody around, just myself."

One night, he saw a shimmering form. "Take a good look at me!" the spirit called. "I will give you my power . . . You may think I am nothing! You may think I am only bones! But I am alive!" In one encounter a spirit gave precise instructions for making a light war club. Another "told me never to be mean. Never hurt a dog without cause, to do nothing violent—only as had to be done." He learned songs and was told to keep small charms, all of which would help him to call forth the power he was given.

Yellow Wolf's spirit name was White Thunder, after the power he was given as a warrior to strike enemies like lightning. Joseph once said his name, Hin-mah-too-ya-lat-kekht, was given to him during a vision in the Wallowa Mountains. It was the name of one of his mother's brothers. It too was based on thunder, which symbolizes a mysterious, irresistible force, but not lightning, or white thunder, which was more fitting for a warrior. Joseph's name translates roughly as Thunder in High Mountains.

He once explained to a newspaper reporter, speaking through another Nez Percé man who translated in broken English, that spirits came to his people "and gave them instructions what to do and how to live . . . that these spirits told them to always do what was right toward everyone, that they must stand up for what was right."

But as he grew to manhood and joined his father in trying to cope with dangers his people had never faced before it became increasingly difficult to determine where the right path lay.

4
THINK OF YOUR COUNTRY
Years of Gold and Crisis 1855–71

B y the mid-1850s white settlement in the Pacific Northwest had spread north from the Willamette Valley across
the gently rolling landscape between the Cascade Mountains and the Pacific coast to the shores of Puget Sound. Some
settlers followed a new wagon road from the Oregon Trail up
the Yakima River and through the Cascades to the port town
of Seattle, on the sound. Far to the south, California was a state
of 250,000 people, a market for the Northwest's fish and produce and a source of prospectors looking for the next big gold
strike. Territorial governments had been organized, one for
what is now Oregon state and another for Washington Territory: present-day Washington state, northern Idaho and western Montana.

A few settlers had moved to the old land of the Cayuse near
Fort Walla Walla, and land-hungry whites looked with interest
on the meadows of the Yakima Valley, rolling down the eastern
shoulders of the Cascades. The richest farmland west of the
mountains was taken. Rumors of gold in the Fort Colville area
enticed prospectors. And plans for a transcontinental rail line
through the Northwest sparked dreams of new markets and
rapid settlement.

Isaac I. Stevens, the first governor of Washington Territory,
brought teams of railroad surveyors with him as he traveled
west to take his new post. In 1855, after he had imposed
treaties on the tribes west of the mountains, confining them to
small pieces of land, he turned his attention to clearing the way
for railroads, mines and settlement east of the Cascades.

In the spring Stevens and an Oregon territorial official held
a meeting in the Walla Walla Valley with thousands of Nez

Percé, Walla Walla, Umatilla and Yakima people and the remaining independent Cayuse bands. An estimated 2,500 Nez Percés, probably including Joseph, were there. Stevens brought boatloads of presents and food up the Columbia River for the conference. He explained the government theory of reservations as interpreters called the translations out to the throngs of people.

Hordes of white men were coming, Stevens said, as thick as grasshoppers on the plain. No one could stop them. Some of them were bad men. The Great Father wanted to protect his Indian children, but they must cooperate. They must agree to move onto lands where the government could protect them from the migration. These lands would be set aside, or "reserved," forever for the Indians. If they did not agree, the whites would flood the region and take all the land. Then it would be too late to make room for the tribes. They must act now.

The chiefs had heard stories of war and land grabbing from California and from their old trading partners west of the Cascades. Some of them despised and mistrusted Stevens. Lawyer, the new head chief of the Nez Percés, believed that the only hope Native Americans had for survival was to adopt white ways and to submit to their leadership. A follower of Spalding, Lawyer had taken over the position of head chief after Ellis died in the buffalo country. Lawyer's perceived influence with the powerful officials gave him standing among the Christian Nez Percés of the Clearwater River, who continued to worship and farm as Spalding had taught. Some of the proud buffalo hunting leaders of the tribe disdained Lawyer. Tuekakas and his people in Wallowa Country remained independent as they used cattle to develop their herding economy and became less involved in buffalo hunting. But, like Lawyer, Tuekakas believed trouble with the whites could lead only to disaster.

There was similar diversity of opinion among the other tribes at the council. But Stevens's arguments and implied threats had a powerful affect on them all. If they would agree to move to reserved lands, he said, the government would build houses and mills and shops for them, it would fence and plow fields, send them craftsmen and teachers and livestock and make generous payments to their chiefs. He offered a plan for reservations that effectively split the powerful Nez Percés off from the smaller tribes, giving them virtually all the country they occupied, from the Bitterroot to the Blue Mountains. This included the Wallowa country, virtually all of the extensive Salmon River system and the entire Clearwater system.

With Stevens putting on the pressure and piling on more promises of cash, buildings and livestock, the Yakimas agreed to accept a reservation on the south side of their valley and the remaining tribes agreed to share a reservation in the Umatilla Valley. Each of the chiefs, Tuekakas included, stepped forward as the conference ended to put a mark on the treaty agreement Stevens drew up, signifying consent. The governor promised no one would have to move until the treaty was approved in Washington, D.C., and all the promised work on the reservations had been done.

But Isaac Stevens was a politically ambitious man, anxious to impress the white population. As he had done before with treaties signed by other tribes, he immediately announced that settlers could claim lands given up by the Native Americans. He sent the announcements off to newspapers from the conference grounds and then headed west into the Rocky Mountains to meet with the Salish of Montana, the Blackfeet and other groups along the route he dreamed of for a railroad. Soon the Yakimas, Umatillas, Wallawallas and Cayuse learned from the whites who entered their homelands that Stevens had invited them in.

Violence began first in the Yakima country, as miners moved down the valley toward the Columbia River, which they planned to follow upstream to prospect in the Colville area. A territorial official went in to investigate and was killed. Volunteer troops went in and were beaten by the warriors. Reluctantly, Tuekakas and most of the Nez Percé chiefs agreed with Lawyer that they should not join the Yakimas. When Stevens came to them as he returned from the East, they even agreed to protect him until he could reach territorial soldiers who were moving up the Columbia from the Cascades.

The scope and savagery of the violence that descended upon the other tribes in and around the Columbia Plain over the next four years was unlike anything the Nez Percés had known. Most of the people remained neutral, though a few rode off to join the other tribes, and Lawyer sent warriors to help the white soldiers. In 1856, in the upper Grande Ronde Valley on the doorstep of the Wallowa country, volunteers massacred old men, women and children of the Cayuse and Wallawallas. Tuekakas and young Joseph almost certainly heard first-hand about this from people who managed to escape. Later, federal troops intervened to wage a scorched earth war, burning everything in their path and killing indiscriminately as they marched east across the plains. The Coeur d'Alènes and Spokans were caught up in the war and crushed. Lawyer's men returned to the Nez Percés with stories of warriors hung after they surrendered, villages burned, hostages carried off, food stores destroyed and herds of horses slaughtered. Troops hung men at random, without accusation or trial. In a brutal mockery of the council tradition, one general forced a group of people to meet with him beneath the swinging bodies of their men. It was a spectacle the Nez Percés would remember.

The conduct of both the territorial volunteers and the federal army shocked many Nez Percés, and many were bitter toward Lawyer. But ironically, it added heavy weight to his argument that it was folly to oppose the whites. By the end of 1858, the power of all the tribes in the Pacific Northwest, except for the Nez Percés, had been crushed. The Nez Percé bands waited for word on whether the government had ratified the treaty of 1855, hoping the whites would respect its terms and leave them their country. Settlers, prospectors and speculators poured into the interior of the Pacific Northwest. In 1859 the village of Walla Walla, which had been just a few shacks, grew rapidly as a supply depot and watering hole for prospectors, who thought there was gold in the Blue Mountains to the south.

Wallowa men came in to trade. Alcoholism was rampant among the white population and Native Americans had no resistance to it. "My young men get drunk, quarrel and fight, and I don't know how to stop it," Tuekakas said that summer to the federal Indian agent who had been sent to the Nez Percés. "A great many of my men have been killed by it; and I am afraid of liquor."

This meeting of Tuekakas and other chiefs with the agent was held to announce that the treaty had been ratified, the boundaries of Nez Percé territory would be respected and the mills, houses, goods and cash that had been promised would be delivered. Before this, Tuekakas, had steadfastly refused to take gifts from the whites and warned the Wallowa people not to do so. "He had a suspicion of men who seemed so anxious to make money," Joseph said. The aid called for in the treaty was to go to the Clearwater area, especially Lapwaii. The cash payments were to go to Lawyer. Because the Wallowa Nez Percés had given up no land, Tuekakas reasoned, they should accept no payments.

But, in a speech to the agent in 1859, Tuekakas changed his position in a way that shows he was already concerned that the government might try to make his people leave the Wallowa country. "There is where I live and there is where I want to leave my body," he said. His people should not have to move in with any other bands, Tuekakas argued. "I have a great many bad young men. I don't want them all to live together in one place; it will not do. We have too many horses and cattle to feed on one piece of land . . . If the buildings you spoke of, and are mentioned in the treaty, were divided, it would be better for us all . . . I wish you could arrange it so we could live in our own country."

This put Tuekakas squarely at odds with Lawyer. As head chief, Lawyer's power and credibility among the government-oriented Nez Percés depended on him having influence over who benefited from the government payments, goods and buildings. He became, in effect, a leader whose power depended largely on patronage. He wanted this patronage centralized at Lapwaii under his influence, not divided with the Wallowa Nez Percés. Tuekakas, on the other hand, must have realized that if agency buildings were also built in the Wallowa country, this would help assure that the Wallowa remained part of the reservation.

Lawyer prevailed, but in a few years it became clear that a reservation was a place of confinement and not a protected reserve. The continuing strength and freedom of the Wallowa people became an embarrassment to Lawyer and a beckoning alternative to the path of submission that he followed. At the end of 1859 the prospectors of Walla Walla found that their dreams of gold in the Blue Mountains were illusory. In 1860 one of these men, who had picked up stories from some Nez Percés of shining pebbles in tributaries of the Clearwater, stole with a few friends into the mountainous country around what would soon be known as Oro Fino Creek and found gold deposits.

Soon newspapers proclaimed the news: Gold on the Nez Percé reservation! "What are to be the results of these discoveries?" a Portland newspaper writer asked: "Tremendous stampedes from California to the mines—a flood of overland emigration—a vastly increased business on the Columbia River—the rapid advance of Portland in business, population and wealth—the profitable employment of the farmers . . . these results are certain to follow these great gold discoveries as day is to follow night."

Next spring, the invasion came. Steam-powered paddlewheelers bearing miners, equipment and supplies churned up the gorge of the Columbia River from the Cascades. They passed the hot, arid country of the lower Columbia Plain and climbed into the greener Snake River country. "Gentlemen seated on the forward guard view the scenery, smoke Havana cigars and quaff champagne cocktails," Henry Miller, a newspaper reporter, wrote.

At the mouth of the Clearwater, Miller looked over the bottom land where Lewis and Clark had rested and built dugout canoes on their journey downriver more than 50 years before. "Then," he wrote "in the days of our weakness, we came offering friendship to the natives, and they accepted it, and have kept their part of the agreement; . . . Now the white man comes again to the land of promise . . . He comes in the plenitude of power; armed with all the mechanical appliances to conquer the opposition of nature, and to subdue the poor Indian whose humble supplicant he once was."

By the end of 1861 more rich gold fields had been found in the mountains around the south fork of the Clearwater and in the Salmon River country to the south. In 1862 prospectors struck gold along the Powder River, south of the Wallowa country, and they began to uncover the vast wealth in silver and other minerals of the Boise basin in southern Idaho. That touched off the greatest rush since 1849. Tens of thousands of people stampeded into the Northwest to mine silver and gold and to scour the Rocky Mountains for new riches.

While the Civil War raged, a tide of settlement swept across the Great Plains from the east and rose toward the crest of the Rocky Mountains. It poured through the Cascades from the west, spreading across the Columbia Plain and into the Rockies. It rose all around the Wallowa country: beyond the Seven

Devils peaks to the east, where miners worked the Salmon River country and homesteads and villages sprouted on the prairie nearby; to the south, where a great mining industry flourished on the Snake River Plain and the Oregon Trail bore rivers of people, livestock and supplies; to the west, where farms and ranches covered the broad land of the upper Grande Ronde Valley; and to the north, beyond the deep canyons of the lower Grande Ronde, where cattlemen pastured their herds and steamboats shuttled past the bluffs of the lower Snake River going to and from the new town of Lewiston.

Lewiston, at the junction of the Snake and Clearwater rivers, was about as far upstream as the river boats could safely go. It sprang up almost overnight with a population of thousands. Pack trains fanned out from there and from Walla Walla to the mines. Lewiston and the mines of the Oro Fino, the Clearwater and the Salmon rivers were all on land guaranteed to the Nez Percés under the treaty of 1855. But the federal government, by then preoccupied with the Civil War crisis, made no attempt to halt the invasion and did virtually nothing to protect the Nez Percés. Whether they were Christian farmers or not, they had no legal rights in practice. Farmers and ranchers took land. Rustlers stole stock to sell at the mines. The whites brought alcoholism, prostitution, rape, murder and theft to the Clearwater River and Salmon River Nez Percés, with no interference from the law.

In 1863 the federal government established Fort Lapwaii near the Spalding Mission site and garrisoned it with volunteers from Oregon, since no federal troops were available. That spring officials from Oregon and Washington Territory held a council near the agency with Lawyer and a group of other chiefs. They proposed a new reservation about a tenth the size of the first one. It would include only the lower portion of the Clearwater, where Lawyer and his followers had their farms, and the grasslands southwest of that 100-mile river section.

It is not clear whether Tuekakas or any of the Wallowa Nez Percés attended this council, but there was strong opposition from some of the bands represented. Bands from Salmon River, Hell's Canyon, the Wallowa and the country north of there along the Snake River would all lose their lands. There were also bands living within the proposed reservation who were not loyal to Lawyer and did not want bands from other areas to be penned in with them. Lawyer himself wanted at first only to

The Indian Agency headquarters in Idaho, which was established in the 1860s near the site of the Spalding mission on the Clearwater River. (Courtesy Historical Photograph Collections, Washington State University)

give up land for the mines and for Lewiston. But with the aid of Henry Spalding, who had come to the meeting as interpreter, the officials worked on Lawyer and some of the other chiefs in private. As they came round to support of the new treaty, a bitter dispute grew between pro- and anti-treaty factions.

Word was dispatched to the fort to send in a few troops quietly as a precaution against trouble. Early on the morning of June 5, at about 1 A.M., 20 cavalrymen of the Oregon volunteers rode into the council encampment from the fort. Captain George Currey heard voices in one large compound tipi. Taking an interpreter with him, the captain approached the lodge and listened. A chief named Big Thunder, whose people lived near Lapwaii but had never fallen under Spalding's sway, was one of the most outspoken opponents of the treaty. Currey later recalled:

> The debate ran with dignified firmness and warmth until near morning, when the Big Thunder party made a formal announcement of their determination to take no further part in the treaty . . . and in an emotional manner, declared the Nez Percés nation DISSOLVED; whereupon the Big Thunder men shook hands with the Lawyer men,

telling them with a kind but firm demeanor that they would be friends, but a distinct people . . . I withdrew my detachment, having accomplished nothing but witnessing the extinguishment of the last council fires of the most powerful Indian nation on the sunset side of the Rocky Mountains.

The next day, when the meetings resumed without the anti-treaty chiefs, Lawyer said nothing of the decision that Captain Currey had witnessed. He and his followers agreed to the treaty. Of the 51 men who signed, 49 lived on the new reservation, and two who lived nearby were allowed to keep their homes as private property. Not one leader from any of the dispossessed bands signed.

Based on this document the federal government took 6.9 million acres from the Nez Percés, leaving them with less than 800,000 acres, claiming that those who signed represented a majority of the tribe. Though the chiefs had agreed to accept the position of head chief when White's laws were approved in 1843 they never had any idea that a part of the tribe could sell the lands of the others. The treaty of 1855 had been accepted not merely by some of the bands but by all of them. The U.S. government declared the treaty of 1863 binding in all the bands, whether they had accepted it or not.

Four groups of Nez Percés that lost all or part of their lands under what they called the Thief Treaty of 1863 refused to recognize Lawyer's act as binding on them. They became known as the nontreaty Nez Percés, including the bands from the Wallowa country, Hell's Canyon, the Salmon River and the people of Chief Looking Glass, who lived just inside the southeast boundary of the Idaho reservation, on the Clearwater River. This last group had lost some land under the treaty and refused to accept reservation control. For example, its people did not ask permission from the government agent to travel outside the reserve, as treaty Nez Percés did.

Either at the council or sometime after, Tuekakas angrily spurned the treaty of 1863 and rejected efforts by his old friend, Spalding, to get him to sign. Joseph remembered him saying to Spalding, "I have no other home than this. I will not give it up to any man. My people would have no home. Take away your paper. I will not touch it with my hand."

Tuekakas was amazed and outraged to learn the government nonetheless claimed it had bought the Wallowa country. He destroyed the Bible tract the Spaldings had taught him to read years before and led his men across the gorge of the lower Wallowa River where a trail led to the Grande Ronde Valley, now occupied by white ranchers. Here the men set poles in the ground and built up a stone monument around the base of each pole. The poles formed a line across the trail. Tuekakas said, according to Joseph, "Inside is the home of my people—the white man may take the land outside. Inside this boundary all our people were born. It circles around the graves of our fathers, and we will never give up these graves . . ."

Sometime during these turbulent years Joseph married for the first time. The woman's name, a member of the Wallowa band said years later, was Hy-yum-yu-yik-ty, and she came from the Kamiah area. The Wallowa band made visits every year to Weippe Prairie, near Kamiah, so Joseph may have met her some years before they married. They had a daughter, Khap-khap-onmi, in the mid-1860s.

Other personal details about Joseph's early adult years are scarce. He may have traveled to the buffalo country once with his father. But his main concerns as a young man must have been stock breeding, horse training and hunting in the Wallowa country. It also seems clear, from the ability he later showed in debate and the people's decision to make him chief, that he participated in the long, agonized councils his people must have had to discuss the wars, the gold rush and the treaties of 1855 and 1863.

The fragments of one searing personal experience have come to light. In the later 1860s Joseph's older brother Shugun was killed by a drunken member of the tribe. Joseph, the oldest surviving relative of fighting age, followed custom in seeking justice for a serious crime. He found the killer and shot him, though not fatally. Years later he forgave the man. Joseph once referred to this brother briefly, indicating that he was buried in the Wallowa country.

Soon after Shugun's death, Joseph recalled, "my father became blind and feeble. He could no longer speak for his people. It was then that I took my father's place." A government official described the new chief in a report:

He is in the full vigor of his manhood; six feet tall, straight, well formed and muscular; his forehead is broad, his perceptive faculties large, his head well formed, his voice musical and sympathetic; and his expression usually calm and sedate; when animated, marked and magnetic. His younger brother [Ollokot] in whose ability he evidently confides—putting him forward much of the time as his advocate—is two inches taller than himself, equally well formed, quite as animated and perhaps more impassioned in speech . . .

Besides sharing Joseph's responsibilities, Ollokot—a daring rider and expert with guns—was leader of the band's warriors.

Soon Tuekakas's condition worsened, and Joseph made him a deathbed promise that would haunt the son the rest of his life. It happened in the late summer or fall of 1871, as they camped in the broad central portion of the Wallowa valley, near bubbling springs that watered the land between the forks of the Wallowa and Lostine rivers. The people had been catching salmon through the late summer and would soon head into the southern mountains to hunt. Joseph remembered:

My father sent for me. I saw he was dying. I took his hand in mine. He said: "My son, my body is returning to my mother earth, and my spirit is going very soon to see the One Above. When I am gone, think of your country. You are the chief of these people. They look to you to guide them. Always remember that your father never sold his country. You must stop your ears whenever you are asked to sign a treaty selling your home. A few years more and the white men will be all around you. They have their eyes on this land.

"My son, never forget my dying words. This country holds your father's body. Never sell the bones of your father and your mother." I pressed my father's hand and told him I would protect his grave with my life. My father smiled and passed away to the spirit land.

I buried him in that beautiful valley of winding waters. I love that land more than all the rest of the world. . . .

5

I WISH YOU COULD HAVE SEEN THEM
Chief Joseph and the Flowering of the Wallowa Nez Percés 1871–75

In less than a decade after settlers moved into the Grande Ronde country, pastures there began to give out. Drought brought the problem to a head in 1871, and ranchers began to drive their stock to the lower Wallowa Valley to fatten on the bunch grass that grew thickly there. Some came to cut hay. Fifteen decided to stake claims and made plans to return with their families the following spring.

Settlement of the Wallowa Country brought crisis upon Joseph just as the death of his father took from him his most important guide and teacher. Like any chief, he listened to his people around the council fire, especially to the elders. But more and more, as he faced new and daunting problems that defied traditional answers, Joseph turned to his brother Ollokot as an advisor, a fellow spokesman for the people and as a leader who could maintain the all-important discipline of the warriors. Despite mounting tension, fading hope and ancient traditions that sanctioned violence in defense of their home, the people maintained solidarity behind their chiefs and the policy of peace. The Wallowa warriors, who would later show they could be very dangerous men, harmed no one.

Joseph defied the attempts of a government agent to lure the Wallow band to the Nez Percé reservation in Idaho with presents and promises of support. "Keep your presents," he said.

> We can go to your towns and pay for all we need. We have plenty of horses and cattle to sell, and we won't have any help from you. We are free now. We can go where we

please. Our fathers were born here. Here they lived, here
they died, here are their graves. We will never leave them.

But how could they avoid trouble with the newcomers, trouble that would surely lead to a futile war? Both treaty and
nontreaty groups in Idaho had already seen miners, stock
rustlers, whiskey pedlars and homesteaders take over their
country. They had managed to remain at peace despite numerous provocations, including murder. Having abandoned traditions of group defense and retaliation against wrongdoers,
which would have triggered war, these bands faced a growing
sense of uncertainty and frustration. Alcoholism was rampant.
Treaty chiefs and their followers became dependent on government handouts and fell ever more under government control.

Joseph and his band sought a different path. They waged a
nonviolent struggle against white occupation of the Wallowa and
against the treaty of 1863. Joseph upheld the whites' own concept
of law, both the law people established to live with each other and
a higher law handed down by the Creator. The chief argued from
concepts of property, justice and fairness that whites understood.
He and his people steadfastly practiced peaceful coexistence
while letting it be known they were capable of self defense.

In 1872, as dozens more homesteaders headed for the Wallowa, Joseph and Ollokot sought out the white people to explain
the Nez Percés' claim to the country and ask for a halt to
settlement. They traveled to the Grande Ronde in July. In
August they called a council with settlers in the Wallowa. John
Monteith, who had been appointed agent at the Idaho reservation in 1871, heard of the meetings and made the two-day ride
to the Wallowa to take part.

Monteith was the son of a minister. The Presbyterian Church
had appointed him agent after President Ulysses Grant turned
all reservations in the country over to the major religious
denominations. Grant took this action because political ap-
pointees had become notorious for stealing from the tribes.
From his agency headquarters in Lapwaii, Monteith continued
efforts to move the Nez Percés into agriculture and Christianity. Now, for the first time, he met the man who was emerging
as the most prominent leader of the "heathen" Nez Percés.

Joseph treated whites with respect but showed not the faint-
est sign of awe or fear. He was a large, quiet man, "moderately

This 1879 photo shows John B. Monteith (standing), who became Indian agent at the Idaho Nez Percé reservation in 1871, and three of his Nez Percé followers: Reuben, Lawyer and Billy. (Courtesy Historical Photograph Collections, Washington State University)

tall and heavily built," a woman who met him years later wrote, "hand that felt as big as a ham when shaking hands. Eyes small but particularly bright. At first one doesn't notice his eyes but suddenly you perceive these bright, searching, direct little eyes riveted upon you."

He argued patiently, firmly and without rancor.

> Suppose a white man should come to me and say "Joseph, I like your horses and I want to buy them." I say to him, "No, my horses suit me, I will not sell them." Then he goes to my neighbor . . . My neighbor answers, "Pay me the money, and I will sell you Joseph's horses." The white man returns to me and says, "Joseph, I have bought your horses and you must let me have them." If we sold our lands to the Government, this is the way they were bought.

Joseph Johnson, a settler who spoke the Chinook trade language, served as interpreter between Chief Joseph and the white men in the councils of August 1872. Joseph made clear to Johnson that the Wallowa band would give some land to friendly whites. But they must understand, the chief said, that this country belonged to the Nez Percés.

Johnson and the other settlers at the councils would not concede ownership of the Wallowa to the Nez Percés, but they agreed with Joseph and Ollokot that the government should look into the dispute and come up with a solution. Monteith agreed to pursue this course. He wrote to the Interior Department in support of Joseph: "It is a great pity that the valley was ever opened for settlement. If there is any way by which the Wallowa Valley could be kept for the Indians, I would recommend that it be done."

By then, late in 1872, the number of settlers in the valley had increased fourfold, to about 60. A Grande Ronde man named A. C. Smith, long a friend to many Sahaptin bands, was building a bridge across the canyon of the lower Wallowa River and a wagon road into the valley. In December Joseph and Ollokot stopped by Smith's bridge project on their way to the Umatilla country. They had objected strongly to the bridge but were still good friends of Smith. They stayed and had lunch with him. Some weeks later a Grande Ronde newspaper, *The Sentinel*, reported that Joseph and his entire band had descended upon Smith "and had been very saucy and indicated a desire to cause trouble."

Joseph continued discussions with white officials in March 1873 at Lapwaii and seemed to make progress. Monteith and an Interior Department Indian commissioner inclined to the view that the government could buy the settlers out and establish a Wallowa reservation. They agreed to explore the prospect even when Joseph said he did not want schools or churches on the projected reservation because "they will teach us to quarrel about God, as the Catholics and Protestants do on the Nez Percés reservation and at other places . . . We may quarrel with men sometimes about things on this earth, but we never quarrel about God. We do not want to learn that."

In April the Interior Department banned settlement throughout the area drained by the Wallowa River and ordered appraisal of the settlers' holdings for purchase by the government. This action left Indian haters in the Grande Ronde sputtering with fury. "The Wallowa Gone," *The Sentinel* headline read, "Dirty, Greasy Indians to Hold the Valley; Two Hundred White Men, and Families Driven from the Beauty

Spot of Oregon to Make Room for About Forty Accursed Indians; Citizens of Wallowa! Awake and Drive Joseph and His Band from the face of the Earth." At this time there were fewer than 90 settler households in the Wallowa, along with large herds belonging to ranchers who lived in the Grande Ronde, and about 300 Nez Percés.

The prospect of Oregon's northeast corner being set aside for Indians quickly became a hot political topic across the state. Now Governor Leonard F. Grover pressed the Interior Department to abandon the reservation plan. In a letter of July 1873, he wrote to the department that the Wallowa country was "the key" to all eastern Oregon and that if the whites were "removed to make roaming ground for nomadic savages, a very serious check will be given to the growth of our frontier settlements and to the spirit of our frontier people." The government should stick to a policy, he added, of removing Indians "to make way for civilization."

After announcement of the Interior Department's decision, settlement of the Wallowa came almost to a halt, though large herds of Grande Ronde cattle continued trailing in and out. Appraisers arrived in July to assess the value of the white people's properties and left. Soon after an order came from President Grant declaring a reservation in all of the Wallowa country except the southern end. The high southern mountains and the sacred and bountiful Wallowa Lake were *outside* the reserve; most of the white homesteads to the northeast in the middle and lower Wallowa Valley, were *inside*.

As fall came on the government did nothing, leaving both Nez Percés and settlers confused. That November, during one of his frequent visits to the reservation in Idaho, Joseph asked Monteith to get him permission to travel to Washington, D.C., and meet with the president. Monteith reported the request but did not push for it. He had begun to worry that the nontreaty chiefs, particularly Joseph, were undermining the authority of the treaty chiefs and the government among the Nez Percés. The nontreaty Nez Percés often mingled with their treaty relatives, especially at the annual root digging festivals that continued on Weippe Prairie east of Kamiah on the Idaho reservation. People in the treaty bands saw the independence of all the nontreaty Indians and particularly the fine horses, cattle and traditional dress of the Wallowa band. They saw the nontreaty bands run their own affairs in councils and uphold their own values and spiritual life in their own religion.

An army officer's wife who generally despised Native Americans and who wished "somebody would kill" Joseph could not help being impressed by him and three other men who rode into Fort Lapwaii one rainy day in November 1876. Emily Fitzgerald wrote to her mother:

Positive identification is not possible, but there is evidence suggesting that the woman on the right is Joseph's daughter Khap-khap-onmi. On the left is one of Joseph's two sisters who lived on the Idaho Nez Percé reservation. Note that Joseph's sister has adopted a white style of dress while his daughter prefers a more traditional style. (Courtesy Historical Photograph Collections, Washington State University)

I wish you could have seen them. You never saw such style
. . . We all stood in the rain, as we hadn't seen such
gorgeous array before. One of them who did most of the
talking had a headpiece for his horse that covered his
horse's whole head. It was just covered with beads. There
were holes for the eyes, and it was really very showy. His
own costume was of some kind of skin trimmed in ermine.
A fringe of ermine skins (whole skins) was around the
jacket and about the knees, and down the seams of the
sleeves from shoulder to waist, and around his cap. Their
faces were all painted, and all had bows, and quivers of
arrows slung at their backs. The quivers were all highly
ornamented with beads . . . They were all very smiling and
pleasant . . .

The Wallowa Nez Percés did not wither during the twilight
years in their homeland, they flourished. Yellow Wolf fondly
remembered as an old man the days of his youth in the Wallowa
Valley and the high mountains to the south. "We would go to
Wallowa in the spring for salmon," he said, "stay there all
summer and until late fall. Plenty of game. It was easy to get
our winter's food . . . We were raising horses and cattle—fast
race horses and many cattle. We had fine lodges, good clothes,
plenty to eat, enough of everything. We were living well."

Visitors and settlers in the Wallowa country who wrote down
their impressions estimated the band had upwards of 4,000
horses. The cattle were more spread out, and no one tried to
count them. But there were more than the entire band could
round up in a month. As settlement and trade increased around
the Wallowa Nez Percés, the value of their livestock rose. They
could afford to buy ample stocks of metal tools, silverware,
utensils, weapons, tobacco, coffee, sugar, flour and glass beads.
They accumulated considerable fortunes in gold. Women continued to develop the beauty and intricacy of their arts and
crafts.

More than showing off their finery, the Wallowa Nez Percés
joined with other nontreaty bands to reaffirm and reshape
their people's traditions as an alternative to the path of the
treaty chiefs and the white people. Elizabeth Wilson, a Nez
Percé born in 1882 in the mountainous country of the middle
Clearwater, heard about this from her mother and other elders.
They had seen the annual gatherings of treaty and nontreaty

bands at Weippe Prairie during the 1870s. A group from White Bird Creek in the mountains and canyons of lower Salmon River camped near Joseph's people at Weippe. Wilson named a dozen more bands that came every year.

> One thing that the people of Joseph's band and of the White Bird band always held is the religious observance of turning-around-oneself (Dreamer Religion). They never failed to hold the ceremony day after day. Early in the morning they were off to dig. The women dug, until after noon, then in the afternoon went home. They cleaned themselves, bathed, and got dressed up in the Indian dress. Then they went to the Indian religious services. They heard the drum going, "pim, pim." Then they started, the believers of that religion raised their heels . . . This dream or something used to teach them the song. It used to give them something. And this was the land they had. And they sort of worshipped the sun. Then they were given more visions. There was one thing more powerful which ruled everything, the earth and the sun . . .
>
> And there was another thing that these Indian worshipers did. They had no rubbish outside. The earth was theirs and they always kept it clean. They said [they did this] because "we respect the earth." Because they worshipped the earth, the sun and furthermore whatever is higher up, they used to have respect for the earth. They never left anything lying around untidy, and that is the way these worshipping Indians took care.

In their idea of a single God—"one thing more powerful which ruled everything"—the Dreamers countered the idea that the red-skinned people were somehow inferior to whites and should follow them. Joseph championed the belief that children of one Creator must be of equal worth.

To white officials like John Monteith, Dreamers were all followers of Smohalla, a religious leader among the Palouse who prophesied that all the whites would disappear. Nez Percé Dreamers did not follow any particular prophet or cult and they did not accept Smohalla's prophecies. They continued in the spiritual beliefs of their ancestors, which had always included belief in the significance of dreams. It was probably after contact with Christianity—although no one can tell for sure—

that they developed ideas about a single God. They called this Ah-kun-ken-ekoo, Land Above or One Above.

All this was intolerable to Monteith, who came to believe that Joseph and the non-Christian Nez Percés were subversives. A supporter of the Wallowa reservation plan when he was a new agent in 1872, over time Monteith turned away from it and from Joseph until finally he committed himself to ending the freedom of the nontreaty bands. In 1872 Monteith wrote that the Wallowa Valley was unsuitable for agriculture and should be left to the Nez Percés. In 1874 he claimed that he had never favored a reservation there unless Joseph's people agreed to farm that land. "Joseph and his band are not entitled to the Wallowa unless they go there and settle down," he wrote. "The only thing that can be done with these Indians is to compel them to remain in one place or the other and to accomplish this force will be necessary. These non-treaty chiefs will take nothing from any government officer not even beef which I have offered several times only to be refused."

Monteith objected only to Native Americans moving about. He had no objection to white people wandering where they pleased. Wallowa settlers often left their homes for months at a time, traveling to work the harvest season in farming areas like the Walla Walla country, taking jobs in mills and taking children to live near schools.

After Grant's order for a reservation came out in mid-1873, the uncertainty continued for about two years. As spring 1874 came on, Monteith warned of possible trouble. Troops moved into the Wallowa Valley from Fort Walla Walla that June but found the Nez Percés had not yet come in from the canyons and forests to the north. The band had trailed north to the Snake River and east across the Idaho reservation to Weippe Prairie. There Joseph and Ollokot held a council with leading chiefs and fighting men of the nontreaty bands. They agreed they could not gain anything by going to war.

Joseph and his band returned to the Wallowa Valley in the summer of 1874, and they had no trouble with the settlers. Though the reservation plan appeared doomed, Joseph stuck to the strategy of maintaining order, cultivating goodwill and making his case to settlers and the government. But the next spring, in 1875, President Grant formally rescinded his order for a Wallowa reservation; again Monteith called for troops.

The valley remained calm. Joseph or Ollokot (it is not clear which, because the settlers sometimes mixed the brothers up) saved a white woman and her daughter from drowning in the swollen Wallowa River. When Captain Stephen G. Whipple arrived with troops he found no sign of tension on either side. Joseph, he wrote, "and several other leading Indians spoke of the bitter disappointment to them that this valley was thrown open to settlement after it had been for so long a time understood that it should be reserved to them; but that under the circumstances the Indians desired to share it with the white people . . . I believe they honestly mean to avoid all cause of trouble with their white neighbors . . ."

Later in that summer of 1875 the chiefs invited another officer to a festival where more than 500 people from Nez Percé and other tribes gathered at the forks of the Wallowa and Lostine rivers, right in the middle of the white settlements. The people were relaxed and friendly, the officer reported. "The white settlers of the valley passed back and forth through the Indian camp with a feeling of perfect safety." The nontreaty chiefs held council again, this time by the Wallowa River, and again they affirmed their commitment to peace. Whipple's men began to joke that they would gladly spend their summers in the peaceful land of winding waters, feasting on salmon and game.

When a notice came from Monteith ordering Joseph to take his people to the reservation in Idaho, Whipple informed Joseph and reported,

> he asked earnestly if I had nothing more to say, to which I replied in the negative. He looked disappointed, and after a short silence he said he hoped I could tell something of a possible doubt of their being obliged to relinquish this valley to the settlers. I told him the case was decided against the Indians by higher authority than that of any Army officer. This declaration did not make the countenance of the Indians more cheerful.

Still there was no sign of hostility. The Nez Percés remained friendly but would not pack up and move to Idaho. Whipple, as he continued to deal with Joseph to resolve minor disputes over grazing rights, became an advocate on his behalf. "This band of Indians are by no means a vagabond set," he wrote in a report. "They are proud-spirited, self-supporting and intelligent."

Once again, a powerful white leader began to wonder why the government was courting trouble in the Wallowa country. Just as Monteith raised doubts in 1872 about allowing settlers into the Wallowa, Brigadier General Oliver O. Howard, commander of the army in the Northwest, read Whipple's reports in 1875 and concluded, "I think it a great mistake to take from Joseph and his band of Nez Percés Indians that valley."

Howard was a devoutly religious man who had fought his way across the South with General William T. Sherman in the war against slavery. He had lost an arm in the war. In its aftermath he had coordinated efforts of the Freedmen's Bureau to help the freed slaves get a start under the wartime amendments to the U.S. Constitution. He had helped found a university for African Americans in Washington, D.C., named Howard University in his honor. He considered himself a protector of downtrodden people of color, but he also had a condescending, racially tainted attitude toward them.

Howard ordered an evaluation of the Treaty of 1863 by Major Henry C. Wood, a lawyer on his staff. Wood concluded that "the non-treaty Nez Percés cannot in law be regarded as bound by the treaty of 1863; and in so far as it attempts to deprive them of a right to occupancy of any land its provisions are null and void." Howard persuaded authorities in Washington to form a commission that would try to resolve the problem with the Nez Percés. Joseph understood this to mean that his people would get a full hearing on the issues and a fair decision on the merits. But it seems that Howard merely thought of the commission as a mechanism for buying out the land claims of the nontreaty bands.

Whatever his intentions for the commission were, events overtook Howard quickly in 1876. In the face of mounting pressure to dispense with Native Americans in the interest of "civilization," he caved in. The hardened freedom fighter became, like Monteith before him, a bitter enemy of the nontreaty Nez Percés and a tool of the Indian haters.

6

LAW OF THE EARTH
A Fight for Law and Order
1876 – June 15, 1877

As the spring sun began to warm southern hillsides and canyon walls early in 1876, the Wallowa Nez Percés moved south from their winter home on the lower Grande Ronde River and spread out in search of food. They harvested biscuit root from places the sun touched most, enjoying the first fresh food of the year. As spring wore on the people moved up to the gently rolling section of plateau that lies south of the canyons. Here they camped in June, and the women dug roots while small parties of men went off in search of deer.

It was much the same as any other spring within living memory, except that the Wallowa people had begun the last full cycle of the seasons in their home. The final confrontation began that spring in 1876, when a white man lost some horses and concluded that someone had stolen them. On June 23 H. Findley and Wells McNall, two settlers who later said they were looking for lost horses, met a group of Nez Percé hunters and killed one of them, Wilhautyah, with a rifle.

Settlers in the area holed up in a cabin, fearing retaliation, but none came. Joseph traveled to Lapwaii in July to meet with Monteith and let him know that his people would remain at peace. He returned to the reservation agency late in July with Ollokot and several dozen of the band to meet with Major Wood, who had done the report for Howard concluding that the Wallowa Nez Percés still had a right to their country. Joseph addressed the officer as "my friend," Wood wrote, and said "that it was true one of his brothers had been killed by whites in the Wallowa Valley . . ."

Joseph said that among the Indians the chiefs controlled the members of their bands, and had power to prevent bad Indians from doing wicked things and in case of their so doing to punish them; and if the chiefs did not restrain or punish bad Indians, they themselves [the chiefs] were responsible for their bad acts; and he reasoned that those in authority over the whites had or should have the same control over their men; and hence the white authorities in the vicinity of Wallowa Valley and elsewhere were directly responsible for the killing of his brother . . . that the value of his life could not be estimated . . . that now, since the murder had been done; since his brother's life had been taken in Wallowa valley, his body buried there, and the earth there had drunk up his blood, the valley was more sacred to him than ever before, and he would and did claim it now as recompense for the life taken; that he should hold it for himself and his people from this time forward forever, and that all the whites must be removed from the valley.

Wood listened to Joseph and informed him that a special commission would be appointed to settle all the issues between the whites and the Wallowa Nez Percés. The chief and his people left under the impression that they would be able to pursue their case in an impartial forum and that the government would bring Findley and McNall to justice.

Late in June, within days of Wilhautyah's murder, the Sioux crushed George Custer and his men of the 7th Cavalry at the Little Big Horn River in eastern Montana. Commentators and politicians eulogized the general, who had earned the name "Squaw Killer" from the Sioux, as a noble hero cut down by red demons. Armies converged on the northern plains and hunted the Sioux through summer, fall and winter. A cry rose in the Pacific Northwest to round up and confine every last band of Native Americans.

Joseph and Ollokot kept their people away from the settlers and grew ever more fearful and angry as white authorities took no action against Findley or McNall, as more settlers moved in, and no word came on the commission that Colonel Wood had promised. Late in August, Joseph became the only leader on either side to attempt an investigation.

There had been no friction between the Findleys and the Nez Percés before the killing of Wilhautyah. One evening Joseph rode over to Findley's house alone to talk to him about the incident. He returned for two more interviews. He did not visit McNall, who had a history of hostility toward the Nez Percés. The chief concluded that both men were responsible for the murder, though Findley was the one who did the shooting. More importantly, he held the whites in general responsible for tolerating what they would not have tolerated had the victim been one of them. Early in September the Wallowa Nez Percés ordered the whites to surrender Findley and McNall to them and to leave the country. The whites refused. Joseph and Ollokot then gave them one week to leave or be forced out.

Word of the confrontation reached the Grande Ronde Valley where, despite the harvest season, 40 armed men were soon on their way to the Wallowa Valley. The news also reached Fort Walla Walla and troops marched off behind the volunteers.

Joseph and Ollokot waited out the week they had given for the settlers to leave. They began moving their people from the forks of the Lostine and Wallowa to a more isolated campground at the lake. They posted small groups of men at key points to keep an eye on the valley. On September 8 one of these scouting parties encountered an Indian hating settler, Gerard Cochran, who boasted that men from the Grande Ronde were coming, ready to fight. Cochran threatened to kill and scalp Chief Joseph.

The next day, Saturday September 9—the last day before Joseph had said the settlers must leave—about 70 Nez Percé men galloped their horses up to a ranch on Alder Slope, just northwest of Lake Wallowa at the foot of the southern mountains. There they found Cochran with several families. The warriors were stripped to the breechclout and painted for battle except for one, Joseph. A group of women leading pack horses came in behind them. As the Native Americans and settlers faced each other, the Nez Percé women pointed to the white women and motioned them to take the children and move away from the men. Cochran crept into the barn and hid under a haystack.

With the help of a white who was known to the Nez Percés as a friend and a reliable interpreter, Joseph convened a simple court. He again ordered the settlers to leave the valley, and they quickly agreed to go. Then he called for Cochran, who was dragged from the barn by his neighbors and brought before the chief. In an account of the incident compiled from the stories of the settlers "Joseph held a long club" over Cochran and wanted to know whether this man had lied about the Grande Ronde men coming over and also wanted to know what was this about scalping him. He [Cochran] denied having said it. But the Indian to whom he had said it was standing close by. He [the Indian] promptly told him he was a liar and slapped him. Then the man's father told Joseph that if he would let his son go he would take him out of the country at once. Joseph agreed . . .

The Nez Percés left and Lieutenant A. G. Forse arrived a few hours later, in the early morning hours of Sunday, with 47 cavalrymen. He had overtaken the Grande Ronde volunteers and put them under his command. Forse later reported that one of the witnesses to the confrontation with the Nez Percés "said he did not hear any threats made against those people, but he did hear Joseph say that if the Grand Ronders wanted to fight he would meet them . . . about a mile this side of his [Wallowa Lake] camp on a bluff and would be ready for them all day."

The next day Forse rode out toward the lake with two settlers for interpreters and no troops. A messenger met them and took them to the warriors, who were mounted with guns at the ready. Forse met with a chief he identified as Joseph, though it was probably Ollokot. Ollokot told Forse the band had been waiting for the commission that had been promised them by Colonel Wood, but one of the band had just been at Lapwaii and found that there was still no word of it there. The officer assured the chief that McNall and Findley would stand trial and that the Grande Ronde men would withdraw. He said that while the band awaited the commission it must avoid friction with whites and stay away from the settled areas. "To all of which," Forse reported,

> [Ollokot] said he would agree, and to show his good faith he said he would throw away the bullets they had put in their guns for the purpose of killing the whites who had come to kill him, which he did by forming his Indians in single rank, and discharging their pieces, after which I left him . . .

The People headed back to the lower Grande Ronde for the winter, still determined to remain in their home. Finally, in

Joseph's younger brother Ollokot was leader of the Wallowa Nez Percé fighting men and often represented the band in dealings with government officials. This photograph was taken early in 1877. (Courtesy Historical Photograph Collections, Washington State University)

November, Joseph and Ollokot heard that the commission they hoped would vindicate their claim to the Wallowa had arrived at Lapwaii. Joseph crossed the Grande Ronde and traveled to the agency with about 60 people to meet with the commission, which included Howard, Major Wood and three well-dressed businessmen from the eastern United States. The meeting began in the largest building at Lapwaii, filled with the Wallowa people and Nez Percés from the reservation. Joseph was shocked to find that the commission had already decided against him and his people. They must give up their country and move to the reservation in Idaho, said David H. Jerome, chairman of the commission.

For three tense days Joseph argued for his people's home. The commission reported him as saying:

> He was made of the earth and grew up on its bosom. The earth, as his mother and nurse, was sacred to his affections, too sacred to be valued by or sold for silver and gold. He could not consent to sever his affections from the land that bore him. He was content to live upon such fruits as the "Creative Power" placed within and upon it . . . The earth carried chieftainship [which the interpreter explained to mean law, authority, or control], and therefore to part with the earth would be to part with himself or with his self-control. He asked nothing of the President. He was able to take care of himself.

Quoting Joseph directly, the report continued:

> "We are not to be trampled upon and our rights taken from us. The right to the land was ours before the whites came among us; white men set such authority aside. If that course were adopted neither [side] would have chiefs—neither would have rest. It ought to fill you with fear . . . The earth and myself are of one mind. The measure of the land and the measure of our bodies are the same. Say to us, if you can say it, that you were sent by the Creative Power to talk to us. Perhaps you think the Creator sent you here to dispose of us as you see fit. If I thought you were sent by the Creator I might be induced to think you had a right to dispose of me. Do not misunderstand me, but understand me fully with reference to my affection for the land. I never said the land was mine to do with it as I chose. The one who has the right to dispose of it is the one who has created it. I claim a right to live on my land, and accord you the privilege to live on yours."

"Haven't you a stronger affection for peace than for the land?" Jerome asked.

> "I look upon the land, made as it was, with pleasure. It was made for us, with all its natural advantages . . . There is nothing should supersede it. There is nothing which can outstrip it. It is clothed in fruitfullness. In it are riches

given me by my ancestors . . . I have already shown you
my mind . . . You know what I think as well as I do.
Mr. Jerome. "What shall we say to the President when
we go back?"
Young Joseph. "All I have to say is that I love my
country."

Joseph told the commission that the whites must leave his
country for tolerating murder. As for Findley himself, the chief
said, "I pronounce the sentence that he shall live."

*This photo, taken in 1877 at Bismarck, North Dakota, a few
weeks after the battle of Bear Paws, is one of the first known
pictures of Chief Joseph. He wears a chief's sash. Just below
his right temple, a minor bullet wound has almost healed.*
(Courtesy Historical Photograph Collections, Washington
State University)

The white commissioners could not budge Joseph. They concluded that his "alertness and dexterity in intellectual fencing" were "quite remarkable." They recommended that the government place the Wallowa band on the Idaho reservation—by force if necessary. Howard, like Monteith before him—had turned against the People. Only Wood opposed the commission's decision.

During the winter months an emergency council was held in the secluded reaches of the lower Salmon River among leaders of the four nontreaty bands. Among those present were Joseph and Ollokot of the Wallowa Nez Percés; Chief White Bird of the scattered Salmon River groups; Tool-hool-hool-zote, whose people inhabited the isolated country between the lower Salmon and the Snake rivers; and the people of Chief Looking Glass, who lived near the forks of the Clearwater River's middle and south branches. They agreed to stand together, to stay at peace but not to submit to Monteith's control.

Early in 1877 Joseph refused another demand from Monteith to move to the reservation and Monteith turned the matter over to the military, saying all the nontreaty bands must be brought to heel. Ollokot, acting while Joseph was ill that spring, held a series of meetings with Howard, one of his aides and Monteith, trying to get them to reconsider and assuring them that the band did not want war. "I have a wife and children, cattle and horses," he told the reservation agent. "I have eyes and a heart, and can see and understand for myself that if we fight, we would have to leave all and go into the mountains." The best he could get was Howard's agreement for a council with all the nontreaty bands.

Late in April 1877, the bands traveled slowly over icy mountain trails and converged on the warming Lapwaii Valley. As they turned up Lapwaii Creek on May 3 for a peace council at the fort, the Wallowa people did not know that Howard was moving Gatling guns toward their families in the winter camp they had just left. A precursor of the machine gun, the Gatling could mow people down like grass.

Howard waited for the Wallowa Nez Percés. "At last they came," he wrote,

> riding slowly up the grassy valley, a long rank of men, all
> on ponies, followed by the women and children. Joseph and

Ollokot rode side by side. The faces of all the Indians were painted bright red, the paint covering the partings of the hair, the braids of the warriors' hair tied with strips of white and scarlet. No weapons were in sight except tomahawk pipes and sheath knives in their belts. Everything was ornamented with beads. The women wore bright colored shawls and skirts of cotton to the top of their moccasins.

They all came up and formed a line facing our square enclosure; then they began a song. The song was wild and shrill and fierce, yet so plaintive at times it was almost like weeping, and made us sorry for them, although we could not but be glad that there were not five hundred instead of fifty [warriors].

They turned to the right and swept around outside our fence, keeping up the strange song all the way around the fort, where it broke up into irregular bubblings like mountain streams tumbling over stones.

As far as Howard was concerned, there was nothing to discuss except where the different nontreaty bands would locate on the Idaho reservation. Tool-hool-hool-zote, who argued with him, was seized and thrown into the guardhouse. Bluntly, Howard told the remaining chiefs they must move to the reservation or else face his guns.

Joseph, White Bird, Looking Glass and some others rode over the reservation with Howard for three days, looking for land to move their people to. Then Howard issued them passes and an ultimatum: They had 30 days to go back to their homes and collect their stock and move onto the reservation. They had come to the meeting free people. Now they were reservation Indians who had to have written permission to leave their reserve. From the Wallowa country, where he had gone to check on livestock, Ollokot now rushed word to Joseph at Lapwaii that Howard's cavalry and Gatling guns were near the winter camp of the band.

In vain Joseph pointed out that the rivers were dangerously swollen with spring snow melt. Howard insisted on 30 days, he said. "If you are not here in that time, I shall consider that you want to fight, and will send my soldiers to drive you on." He did not reconsider, even when he heard one of his own men had just drowned trying to cross the Grande Ronde.

Nez Percé families did cross flooding rivers in buffalo hide boats pulled by strong horses. But moving all their stock across meant taking heavy losses, especially of colts, calves and grown cattle. The band would not be able to leave some stock and pick it up when the rivers fell that summer. All animals left behind, Howard said, would belong to anyone who found them.

The greatest loss of all was the loss of the country that held the bones and spirits of the people's ancestors, parents and children. By this time Joseph had buried his mother, his father and several children there. One of the early white settlers remembered the burial of a son of the chief at the foot of Wallowa Lake. Sometime before 1877, it is not clear when, Joseph married a second wife, Toma Alwawinmy. Where she came from is not known. Of the five girls and four boys born to Joseph and his wives, all but a newborn girl and Khap-khap-onmi, a daughter of about 12, lay buried in Wallowa by mid-1877.

Along with his own sorrows, Joseph bore the brunt of his people's fury. Though there was no practical alternative, the decision to give up their home and accept the control of Monteith on the reservation was an agonizing one. Howard's flaunting of force and his refusal to allow time for the river waters to subside all suggested an intent to demean the nontreaty bands and reduce their herds. Some of the young Nez Percé men longed to give Howard his war.

Joseph and Ollokot endured a bitter council with their people, and the decision was made. "We gathered all the stock we could find, and made an attempt to move." Joseph said. "We left many of our horses and cattle in Wallowa, and we lost several hundred in crossing the river. It is still our land. It may never again be our home, but my father sleeps there, and I love it as I love my mother. I left there hoping to avoid bloodshed."

They climbed from the Snake River gorge to the remote highlands between the Snake and the Salmon rivers. Then, leaving some of their cattle behind to graze, they made a second dangerous crossing of the Salmon River and climbed again into the wide prairie south of the reservation. It was early June, the camas beds were ready for digging, and there was still time before the mid-month deadline for moving to the reservation. The nontreaty bands gathered, as the bands had for generations, to dig roots, race horses and hold councils. Many angry words were spoken over more than a week of discussion. The Salmon River Nez Percés bore the shame of many unavenged killings, not just one like the Wallowa band. "They had been insulted a thousand times," Joseph said. "Their fathers and brothers had been killed; their mothers and wives had been disgraced . . . They were homeless and desperate." But war would be fruitless, Joseph and others argued. "We had many grievances," he said. "But I knew that war would bring more."

Joseph remained committed to peaceful resistance. He planned to go to the reservation, visiting the Wallowa country every year as the government had to allow by treaty, and continuing the peaceful struggle to regain his country. This might have been the only logical strategy, but it could not ease the pain of people giving up their homes and accepting the status of inferior beings penned up on a reservation. Some, in their anger, reviled Joseph and other peace advocates as cowards and apostles of submission. Still, after days of talk "I thought the danger was past," Joseph said. At the very least, the chiefs had argued, the people should go to the reservation and wait for the return of two of their strongest war leaders, Rainbow and Five Wounds—who were then in the buffalo country—before even considering war.

On June 12, as the deadline for moving to the reservation neared, Joseph left the camp with Ollokot to recross the Salmon River and butcher cattle. His daughter Khap-khap-onmi, Ollokot's wife Wetatonmi and several others went with them. Joseph's wife Toma Alwawinmi, expecting to give birth any time, stayed behind. They returned after two days with 12 horseloads of meat, intending to pack up and move to the reservation. But as they approached the camp, Wetatonmi said, "we saw a rider coming, running his horse." As he approached them the man called out, "War has broke out. Three white men killed yesterday!" Joseph and Ollokot galloped toward camp. Joseph found himself with a newborn daughter and the apparently unavoidable prospect of war.

"When we reached camp we saw the tipis all down and the horses were being packed," Wetatonmi said. "Chief Joseph and Ollokot rode among the people trying to stop them from moving. They called out to them, 'Let us stay here 'till the Army comes! We will then make some kind of peace with them.' " But few people listened. They knew that 17 men had ridden off to continue the killing. The night before a boy had ridden into camp on the horse of a hated Salmon River white man and announced that the animal's owner was dead. The two killers had camped close by, he said, and would welcome anyone who wanted to join the next day's attacks. Panic swept the camp. The Clearwater nontreaty Indians of Looking Glass and the Palouse wanted no part of the trouble. They packed quickly and headed for their homes on the reservation. Many Salmon River and Hell's Canyon warriors gave in to the longing for revenge. Several of their leading men, believing that war was now certain, consented to lead raids for supplies and weapons. The families of these bands packed and moved northeast to get off the open prairie.

That day the raiders captured large stocks of whiskey. They sank into a drunken frenzy of revenge, first along the Salmon River and several of its side creeks on June 13, then spreading north the next day to Camas Prairie between the settlements of Cottonwood and Mount Idaho. At first they went after known killers, rapists and thieves. Then the raiders turned on anyone not known to be a friend. One of the hardest hit places was the valley of White Bird Creek off the Salmon River, long a home and sacred burial ground to the Salmon River Nez Percés. The homesteads there were laid to waste by the raiders.

"I knew that their acts would involve all my people," Joseph said. "I would have given my own life if I could have undone the killing." He did not think Howard would let his band move peacefully to the reservation even if he could bring himself to abandon the people of White Bird and Tool-hool-hool-zote. The whites knew him as a leader of the Nez Percés' resistance and would turn on him with or without evidence that he had a hand in the violence.

By dawn Joseph and Ollokot had decided that they would not go on the reservation and leave their relatives to the army. The brothers set off with all their family and hundreds of their finest horses to follow their people, on the Long March of the Nez Percés.

7

THUNDER IN THE MOUNTAINS
Expulsion and Defiance
June 16–August 8, 1877

The army first tried to go after Nez Percé families at White Bird Canyon. It is a narrow valley eight miles long, set deep between crowding ridges. Its sides are steep and gullied. The rumpled and broken land of its floor pitches to the southwest, where White Bird Creek flows through a tight gap in the hills to join the Salmon River. The bands chose this place for safety, knowing the army would come. They camped near the foot of White Bird Creek, close to the Salmon River. The chiefs sent scouts into the ridges to watch up the canyon to the northeast and beyond toward Mount Idaho, Grangeville and the road from Fort Lapwaii.

The raiders gathered in after the bands moved south from Cottonwood Creek to White Bird. Stolen goods and whiskey reached the camp. As Captain David Perry closed in with 99 cavalrymen and settler volunteers in the early morning hours of June 17, about half of the 120 to 130 men of fighting age lay insensibly drunk. Scouts spotted Perry in the darkness just before he moved down into the canyon from the northeast. Perhaps 60 men got ready to defend their families. Some, like Joseph, were not warriors or war leaders, but they joined the available fighters to face this emergency.

While they got ready Ollokot told the men they must not shoot first. The chiefs assembled a truce team to ride out to the soldiers under a white flag. The men separated into two groups and moved forward to place themselves between the troops and the tipis, then peered up the canyon in the pre-dawn half-light, searching for the soldiers. A man who went with Joseph and Ollokot remembered that "Joseph said, 'Maybe there are some

Nez Percés with them, and they will tell us if the soldiers are coming with good hearts.' Ollokot looked through field-glasses to see if there were any Indians with the soldiers, and then passed the glasses to Joseph. Two of our men started riding up the hill."

This was the truce team, sent by the chiefs to seek a parley with Perry. The captain, a career officer and Civil War veteran, had brought 10 reservation Nez Percés with him as scouts. But he made no allowance for talks. Moving down the canyon, he put out an advance guard to locate the camp and prepared to charge it at dawn. A settler in the advance opened fire on the truce team, which turned and fled. Perry formed his men into a wide line and tried to advance on the camp. The response came quickly and was so lethal that men on both sides were appalled.

Using the broken landscape for cover, the warriors lunged forward on their best horses. They fell on Perry's line from both ends. Perry's men panicked and fled. While soldiers lashed tired horses up the steep canyon slopes, warriors changed to fresh mounts and pressed the counterattack, dropping the soldiers, as one man remembered "like hunted birds." Thirty-four of Perry's men died. One Nez Percé warrior was seriously wounded but he later recovered. The bands picked up about 60 rifles and plenty of ammunition from the battlefield.

Next morning a small band of Nez Percés just back from a buffalo hunting trip in the northern plains rode into camp with Rainbow and Five Wounds, the great warriors. At a council these men suggested that the bands withdraw across the Salmon River to the mountainous finger of land lying between the Salmon and the Snake river gorges just north of the Seven Devils Mountains. There, they said, the people could stay safely while scouts rode out to Camas Prairie to watch for General Howard. The bands moved up the Salmon the day after the battle to a bend in the river that was a good crossing spot. They passed by the mouth of Slate Creek, where some settlers had gathered for safety at a stockade.

The raiders had done no harm there, for the Slate Creek settlers had bought their land from its original inhabitants and had lived in peace with them afterward. The Nez Percés often traded at the Slate Creek store, many of them on credit. On the day the bands came past and camped at the crossing near the stockade, warriors rode over to settle accounts at the grocery. "The little bills were all paid," said one of the settlers who was in the stockade, "the Indians sending the different sums to settle them by the warriors who came to talk to us. They said they might not come back as there were too many soldiers, but that they would never give up until forced to do so."

Almost a month would pass before the bands had to make a choice between fighting for their country or leaving it in hopes of finding peace. But even on the day after they routed Perry's soldiers, they had begun to contemplate leaving. Different sources have put Joseph on different sides of this decision. He has been reported trying to arrange peace, wanting to stay and fight it out with the army and—by his own account—wanting to leave the region in order to stop bloodshed. Each version of the story may well hold some of the truth. Joseph and all the people were deeply torn by the choices they faced. His thinking may have changed as he groped for possible answers and tried to fulfill his duty to create consensus in the face of an agonizing dilemma. He wanted to stay as close as he could to his Wallowa home, to either die fighting or to gain a peace that at least gave the people of his band as much as they had when the killing started: namely, a home on the reservation with the right to visit the Wallowa country and the ability to continue pressing their claim to the Wallowa peacefully. But war sickened Joseph and threatened the existence of his people. The duty to protect his people's ancient home came into conflict with the duty to protect the people themselves. It should be no mystery that different stories came out of the turbulent, bitter councils that the Nez Percés held as they fought off the army and struggled among themselves to find their way.

U.S. troops converged on the Northwest from around the country in the second half of June while the bands hid out in the mountains, digging pits to store supplies of extra food, clothing and tools. When Howard finally brought an army to the river crossing near Slate Creek at the end of the month, the Nez Percé bands lured him across. They did not even remove a couple of small wooden boats from the crossing, and Howard used them to ferry his men and equipment. Then the bands disappeared to the north as the general labored after them through rain, fog and mud with heavy cannon and a large baggage train. The Nez Percés recrossed the Salmon at the top of its northern swing, where the river turns west toward the Snake. There were no boats for Howard at this spot. On July 2 the bands moved north from the Salmon gorge into Camas Prairie, leaving the general trapped on the other side of the river with about 500 miserable men.

Soon a messenger reached the bands with news of the army's second assault on a Nez Percé encampment, this one a surprise attack on the people of Looking Glass. This chief had broken with the other nontreaty bands when the raiding began. Hoping to keep his people out of war, he had led them to their home on the reservation, at the forks of the Clearwater River's middle and south branches. Howard, believing Looking Glass would soon join the defiant bands, sent Captain Stephen Whipple to "arrest" him and his people. Whipple had written admiringly of the Wallowa Nez Percés in past years. But on July 1 he moved in on Looking Glass soon after dawn and allowed his Indian-hating settler volunteers to open fire on the tipis. A woman, her baby and a man died. The soldiers and settlers drove the people away, looted and destroyed their homes and took most of their horses.

Now Looking Glass, enraged and fearful that without horses his people were vulnerable to another attack, sent word of his plight to the other bands. The people of Joseph, Tool-hool-hool-zote and White Bird may already have been planning to head across Camas Prairie toward the Clearwater, but now this move became an urgent matter. By coming to the aid of Looking Glass and their kinfolk with him, the other three bands would unify the nontreaty Nez Percés and strengthen their hand against Howard.

First they had to move safely across the open prairie with all their families and livestock, past the fortified settlements at Mount Idaho and Grangeville and past Whipple, who had moved to the head of Cottonwood Creek. On July 3 and 4, the warriors established control over the prairie, wiping out a 10-man scouting party of Whipple's and forcing the captain to dig in at Cottonwood. On July 5 the bands moved southeast, staying close to the mountains and ravines near Salmon River, then east and north toward the Clearwater.

The bands went into camp between the tall bluffs of the Clearwater's south branch, on the west side of the river near the mouth of Cottonwood Creek. They were about five miles upstream from the wrecked village of Looking Glass, who immediately joined them with his people. A small band of Palouse people, who had also tried to avoid war but were close to the nontreaty Nez Percés, came in as well.

The Nez Percé people continued to cache goods and supplies and, with the bands united, to consider what they should do. They were on the reservation, defending themselves from attack but not making hostile moves against the lightly defended reservation agency at Lapwaii or against the terrified whites at Mount Idaho, Grangeville and Lewiston. The attack on Looking Glass must have dimmed any remaining hopes that the army would talk peace after its disaster at White Bird. But the strategy the chiefs had adopted there—halting the killing of settlers, talking to the soldiers if possible and fighting or evading them if not—had worked so far. Some of the men who had taken part in the raids worried that they might be handed over to the whites in exchange for peace. These men, therefore, urged the bands to leave the region and strike out for Canada or the northern plains. But, with no threat near, the people did not have to face a decision to leave their homes.

The arrival of Howard on July 9 suddenly confronted the bands with a much different situation. The troops came from the south, moving down the Clearwater River on the east side, rather than approaching from the southwest as the Nez Percés expected. With the river and its wooded bluffs between the Nez Percé camp and his column, Howard did not notice the camp until he had passed it. Moving in from the north, he wheeled his cannon to the bluffs and began lobbing shells at the camp. He was the third army officer to strike at Nez Percé families.

Wetatonmi, one of Ollokot's two wives, remembered how the battle of the Clearwater began on that hot July afternoon.

> After dinner I felt hot and sweaty and went to the river for a cold swim. Just as I got in the water about to my waist, a man came stepping to the bank and said, "We are under a big body of soldiers! An army is approaching on us! Probably a fight will start any minute!"
>
> I got dressed after a quick dip and went back up to the people . . . Soldiers appeared on the mountain about a mile and a half to the north. A puff of smoke was seen, then came a cannon's boom. I saw the warriors stripping for the battle. I saw a bunch of them, mounted and led by Chief

Toohoolhoolzote, run their horses a ways up the river, where they crossed and climbed the mountain to meet the soldiers. Soon there was fighting up there and the guns were heard plainly. It was then that other warriors left the camp, hurrying to join in the battle. They were led by Wahchumyus [Rainbow] . . . They had waited to protect the families, had Toohoolhoolzote and his warriors failed to hold General Howard's army on the mountain flat. Less than 100 warriors in all went up against the enemies. Many of the tribe were not fighters.

Howard had about five times as many men, but he quickly found himself on the defensive as warriors moved up the bluffs and into ravines on either side of his troops. "They had us so penned in for some time that we were by no means sure we would not be 'massacred' as such victories are usually called by our side of the battle," an officer of Howard's wrote. The fighters "crawled up close to our lines and made good bullet shelters of the many stones on our open battleground and did execution from them . . . It was murderous to send those soldier boys, wholly unqualified as marksmen, to meet such deadly riflemen as the Nez Percés were known to be."

The fight continued into the night and resumed the next day. The discipline of the warriors did not waver in the face of cannon and intense rifle fire. They maneuvered around Howard, fought from behind rock shelters, mounted and charged on command, almost capturing the cannon at one point. Joseph did not join in this fight, but stayed near the lines in a rock shelter below the bluffs, listening as older men and warriors held council there as to how to fight the battle. It was clear that the warriors had a good chance of defeating Howard despite the size of his army, but that they risked heavy casualties if they made the attempt. Several warriors had already died and the cost of pressing the attack seemed too high to many of the men, who knew the bands could easily pack up and get away.

A bitter dispute broke out between warriors who wanted to fight and, if need be, die in their country and those who thought it was possible and worthwhile to obtain peace by leaving. The debate at the battlefield became intense on the second day when some of the warriors called for an all-out charge at the soldiers. One man dismissed the idea, Yellow Wolf recalled: "Why all this war up here? Our camp is not attacked! All can

This photo, taken from a cracked glass plate, shows General Oliver O. Howard. (Library of Congress)

escape without fighting. Why die without cause?" This enraged the men who believed they should fight to the death for their land. "Let us quit the fight," one of them said in disgust. He turned to the men who opposed charging the soldiers and said, "You cowards! I will die soon! You will see hardships in bondage. You will have a hard time. Your freedom will be gone. Your liberty robbed from you. You will be slaves!"

Yellow Wolf returned to the fight but, having failed to maintain a consensus about the purpose of the battle, other men began to leave the lines. Later that morning Joseph realized that the Nez Percé force was getting dangerously weak. He ran back to the camp to get the people moving—almost too late. Around the same time that Joseph left the battlefield Howard launched a charge. His men were very lucky that most of the Nez Percé warriors were not waiting for them. The remaining resistance collapsed, and warriors ran down the steep bluffs toward the river, with bullets singing around them. Yellow Wolf was among the last to flee.

"The women, not knowing the warriors were disagreeing, quitting the fight, had no time to pack the camp," he said. "Chief Joseph did not reach them soon enough." The people were able to grab only a few things and fled with the horses down the valley. They left their tipis, some with food still cooking at the fire, and many of their supplies and possessions. Yellow Wolf, lunging down the bluffs as bullets rained around him, found himself almost alone.

> Crossing the river and reaching where the now empty camp stood, I heard a woman's voice. That voice was one of crying. I saw her on a horse she could not well manage. The animal was leaping, pawing, wanting to go. Everybody else had gone. I hurried toward her, and she called, "Heinmot! I am troubled about my baby!"
>
> I saw the baby wrapped in its cradleboard, lying on the ground. I reached down, picked up the cradleboard, and handed it to the woman. That mother laughed as she took her baby. It was the cannon shots bursting near that scared her horse. She could not mount with the little one. She could not leave it there. The woman with the little baby was Toma Alwawinmi [Springtime], wife of Chief Joseph. . . .Chief Joseph left the battlefield ahead of the retreat. Seeing it coming, he hurried to warn the families. He could not leave his wife had he known. The women were all supposed to be ahead.

Howard's men stopped to tend to their wounded and to plunder and burn the camp. The bands rode south to Kamiah and crossed the river next day to Weippe Prairie. They had shot many soldiers, about 40 of them fatally. But four strong warriors were also dead. While scouts watched Howard, the people who wanted to stay and fight had it out with those who did not.

Without unity among the warriors, there was no way to stay. Looking Glass, who had years of experience in the buffalo country and many friends among the tribes of the plains, agreed to lead the bands to the east. If relinquishing their country still did not bring peace, the bands could move to Canada. Moving over the tortuous Lolo Trail with all the families and their horses was an extraordinary measure. But if Howard followed he would have to abandon his big guns and still he would not keep up. The trail was far too rough for

Yellow Wolf, a nephew of Chief Joseph. (Courtesy Historical Photograh Collections, Washington State University)

travois, but the bands had already lost all their poles and a lot of their baggage to Howard. They had plenty of horses along to carry packs. It was midsummer, so the mountains would not be too cold for sleeping in the open.

They would travel more than 1,500 miles in the next two months, searching and fighting to remain free and to live in their own way, and leaving many of their relatives in graves beside the trail.

Joseph accepted the decision to end the bloodshed, though the idea of wandering homeless with his people in far off lands filled him with foreboding. Yellow Wolf remembered that the chiefs hoped that fleeing Idaho and crossing the mountains to Montana would lead to peace and that the government would eventually allow the bands to have a home somewhere:

Before leaving Idaho one of the chiefs—I do not remember which one—had ridden all about our camp announcing, "We may first go to the buffalo country, and then afterwards join Sitting Bull in Canada. Crossing the mountains, leaving Idaho, we will travel peaceably. No white man must be bothered! Only enemies here we fight. Trouble no white people after passing the Lolo into Montana. Montana people are not our enemies. Enemies only here in Idaho."

As the bands moved along the Lolo Trail into the mountains on July 16, rear scouts spotted treaty Nez Percés tracking them for Howard. In fury, the warriors killed two of Howard's scouts—two of their own relations. Howard held back to wait for more troops and plan his pursuit.

The Nez Percés crossed the rugged Lolo Trail from Weippe Prairie to the Bitterroot Valley in 10 days—about 750 people driving at least 2,000 horses over a steeply pitching, ridge-top trail winding up and down over line after line of mountain peaks. Lewis and Clark had come this way in 1806, as the Nez Percés guided them east toward their homes. The route, the explorers wrote, "was through thick woods and over high hills, intersected by deep ravines and obstructed by fallen timber. It crossed abruptly steep hills, then wound along their sides near tremendous precipices, where, had our horses slipped, we should have been lost irrecoverably." The mountains "so completely enclose us that, though we have once passed them, we almost despair of ever escaping from them without the assistance of the Indians . . . Our guides traverse this trackless region with a kind of instinctive sagacity; they never hesitate, they are never embarrassed."

While on the trail the people talked about whether to turn north at the Bitterroot Valley and head straight for Canada or take the more familiar southerly route to the buffalo country. Looking Glass believed there was no urgent need to get out of the United States, while the bands did need to get supplies of buffalo meat for the winter. Joseph supported him because he wanted to stay in remote country, far away from troops and settlers. Turning north would have taken the bands past numerous mining settlements in the mountains of western Montana. During one council Joseph said, "While we were fighting for our own country, there was reason to fight, but while we are here, I would not have anything to say in favor of fighting, for this is not my country. Since we have left our country, it matters little where we go."

The bands drew near the Bitterroot Valley in western Montana on July 26 and confronted an army officer backed by a few soldiers and several dozen settler volunteers who had built a breastwork of logs blocking the trail. The officer, Captain Charles Rawn, demanded that the Nez Percés give up their guns. The chiefs managed to make contact with the volunteers directly and promised them there would be no trouble if the Nez Percés were allowed their traditional right of peaceful passage through the valley. The volunteers agreed, and most of them deserted Rawn. On the morning of July 28 the bands moved onto a high ridge and passed by Rawn's position.

For 10 days the Nez Percé bands moved south up the Bitterroot Valley into the mountains, and on August 7 crossed the Great Divide into the Big Hole Valley and the westernmost reaches of the Missouri River system. The high, broad valley hemmed in by mountains was a favorite resting spot on journeys to and from the Great Plains. Looking Glass planned to stay a few days while the people hunted and cut tipi poles to replace those they had lost in the fight with Howard at the Clearwater River. He was so concerned about keeping peace that he would not send scouts back toward the Bitterroot to watch for soldiers. He feared whites might take this as a hostile sign or that the scouts might start trouble, as the young men had done in Idaho.

"That night," Yellow Wolf said, "the warriors paraded about the camp, singing, all making a good time. It was first since war started. Everybody with good feeling. Going to the buffalo country! No more fighting after Lolo Pass. War was quit. All Montana citizens our friends. This land had belonged to the Flatheads [Montana Salish], our old-time friends . . . It was past midnight when we went to bed."

The people did not realize that the United States was now at war with them. They did not yet fully understand that the soldiers' objective was to kill them, not just to drive them away.

Four days earlier Colonel John Gibbon, acting on orders to keep the Nez Percés from reaching the Great Plains, had marched into Missoula at the north end of the Bitterroot

Valley. Adding settler volunteers to his soldiers, he assembled a force of about 190 men.

As was usual with the army, Gibbon gave high priority to finding Native Americans to help him fight the embattled bands, so he quickly summoned Chief Charlo of the Salish. Thinking that Nez Percés must have scouts out who would spot him in the valley, Gibbon told Charlo to have them all captured and brought in.

"Charlo is a quiet, pleasant-faced Indian, and had very little to say," Gibbon wrote. "What he did say, however, was to the point, and to the effect that he and his people were friends to the whites, but that in the present struggle between them and the Nez Percés he could not take sides, and firmly declined to do what I wished."

One leader of the Bitterroot settlers also decided against helping Gibbon because, he later wrote, it was wrong and extremely dangerous. J. L. Humble, a Civil War veteran and a captain of the Bitterroot volunteers, led his men with the army troops and another volunteer detachment up the valley. The Nez Percés, he said, had "molested nothing." He did not want to attack them, but he did not want to leave his men. As they neared the Divide in the steep mountains Gibbon asked Humble to lead his volunteers forward, locate the Nez Percés and attack.

Humble refused. "I told my men that that was as far as I proposed going," he later wrote, "that I was not out fighting women and children!"

Some of Humble's men joined the other volunteer unit whose captain, John B. Catlin, reluctantly agreed to go with Gibbon, but not as an advance force. Gibbon sent out scouts instead, then moved off after them into the night of August 9, 1877, east over steep, forested ranks of mountains; east toward the Nez Percés and the charge at dawn.

8

CHIEF JOSEPH AND THE WAR
FOR FREEDOM
August 9–November 23, 1877

On August 9, 1877, in the beautiful Big Hole Valley at the foot of the Great Divide, Colonel John Gibbon launched the army's fourth assault against families of the non-treaty Nez Percés. About 90 Nez Percés died on the spot, two-thirds of them women and children.

After the warriors repulsed Gibbon and his troops, the bands moved away with a staggering burden of wounded. Fair Land, one of Ollokot's wives, died in camp the morning after the battle. Others less fortunate survived days and weeks with horrible injuries. But the bands moved on, south and west toward the Great Plains. Weeks later, on September 5, deep in the mountains of Yellowstone National Park and hundreds of miles from Big Hole, a miner taken captive by the bands noticed 16 badly hurt people with them. One of these, he said, did not have long to live.

In the aftermath of the disaster the chiefs appointed a new guide to lead them safely away from settlers and soldiers and to reach the plains and head for Canada. He was half Nez Percé and half French, a younger man who had spent much of his life in Montana and knew the country better than Looking Glass. He had been in the Bitterroot Valley when the bands came there and decided to join them. One of his names, taken from the card game he loved, was Poker Joe.

For Joseph, as for any chief, to see such casualties among his people and to grasp the ferocity of their enemies was devastating. "You are the chief of these people," his dying father had told him years before. "They look to you to guide them." Now, as the braves waged war to clear a path for the families, Joseph

General John Gibbon, who led an attempted massacre of the nontreaty Nez Percé bands at Big Hole, Montana. (Courtesy the Montana Historical Society, Helena)

strove to keep them organized as a people and to keep them moving.

The warriors fanned out for miles all around the bands and had many dramatic confrontations with settlers and soldiers. The women, children and other noncombatants were the core of the resistance. They cooked the food and cared for the wounded. They tended the horses that were vital to the retreat and were placed under tremendous strain in the desperate fighting and long range scouting of the warriors. Joseph had little to do with the fighting or with Poker Joe's choice of the route. He joined the women and children. When a captured soldier escaped from the bands in Yellowstone Park and reached Howard, he told the general that Joseph had fallen far from his position of leadership. The chief, the soldier said, was doing "squaw work." A small boy with the bands remembered years later that Joseph "kept us moving and kept us away from the soldiers." He led and inspired his people in their struggle, and consoled them in their pain. They did not despise him for this, as the white soldier did; they revered him.

With Five Wounds and Rainbow dead at Big Hole, Ollokot too became even more important to guarding the families. He sometimes stayed close by with a small force while other fighters ranged across the country, and he also led the warriors in a daring attack on pursuing troops. Yellow Wolf, a young man who emerged from Big Hole with the honors of an old warrior, scouted far behind the bands, looking for pursuers.

Poker Joe headed the bands south from Big Hole. He took them toward Yellowstone on a route that was long but easily traveled and only lightly settled. It led up the Big Hole Valley to Horse Prairie in western Montana, keeping just east of the mountains that form the Continental Divide. Then they cut back across the Divide and into Idaho, trailing southwest up the Lemhi Valley to the great expanse of the Snake River Plain. There, in remote country, the bands turned east, skirting mountains to their north as they moved toward the wilderness of Yellowstone Park. In the 10 days after Big Hole, despite their wounded, the bands traveled almost 500 miles, nearly twice the distance covered in the 10 days before the battle. Wottolen, a man from the Wallowa country, told how it was done

> From the Big Hole, Chief Hototo [Poker Joe] was the guide and leader of the Nez Percés. He had been all over that country, east and north, and he knew the land and the trails. He understood, and would have the people up early in the morning, and travel till about ten o'clock. Then he ordered a stop and cooking was done while the horses filled upon grass. About two o'clock he would travel again. Kept going till about ten o'clock at night. We had no timepiece but could easily judge our movements. In this way the people covered many miles each sun. They were outdistancing the soldiers, gaining on them all the time. Everybody was glad.

This moving community used the same sort of criers that Bonneville had noticed decades before in the camp of

Tuekakas, only now the news was more serious than notices of missing articles or horse races. Wottolen said:

> . . . an oldlike man who was still strong, made announce-
> ment of all incidents and events each day. All knew him
> and reported to him who had been wounded or killed in
> battle, who was missing or had disappeared. The names of
> all were known throughout the band.

The slow moving wounded left camp first each day, each one with a companion leading the horse. Joseph generally traveled toward the rear of the column, where he must have seen the dozens of old and injured people who, one by one, decided to leave the bands and die by the trail rather than hinder the flight. Most of these people were slain by Howard's scouts, as the general continued his pursuit of the fleeing bands. The general had given strict orders against the killing of the help-less people, yet the killing went on; Howard took no action to prevent it.

Columns of warriors ranged ahead of the bands to crush any resistance they might meet and to find all the horses they could. "While we had many horses, it was good to have fresh ones," Yellow Wolf said. "Best, too, that none be left for sol-diers." The braves could see the results of Big Hole every time they came near the families and saw the wounded and dying people. They killed many of the men they found in their path as the bands marched, but allowed some to escape. Settlers fled or retreated to stockades as word spread of Gibbon's defeat at Big Hole. On August 13 the bands crossed the Great Divide for the second time and entered the country of the Bannock people, who had often fought with the Nez Percés. Some of the Ban-nocks met with the Nez Percés near the village of Junction, and the two sides warily agreed to leave each other alone.

A settler watching from a stockade at Junction described the arrival of the bands: "The hostile Indians struck our valley about 8 o'clock on the morning of the 13th and continued coming all day . . . They must have had 2,000 head of horses but they are getting worn down and look very thin. The Bannocks say that they have quite a number of wounded with them."

The Nez Percés passed Junction peacefully and moved up the valley. They crossed a gentle divide where the valley begins to slope to the south and Birch Creek runs toward the Snake River Plain.

The bands headed east, quickly now across the plain. They tore down telegraph wires, took horses and horse feed and destroyed harnesses at a stagecoach station. Howard tried to cut them off by taking a shortcut through more settled areas but he was not fast enough. On August 18, nine days after they had staggered south from Big Hole, the bands camped at Camas Meadows on the approach to Yellowstone in eastern Idaho. From a mountain peak to the northwest, Howard's scouts looked out over the flat landscape and could see the bands ahead of them. Howard took up the pursuit. "I am confident . . . we may yet capture or destroy this most enterprising band of Indians," he cabled his superiors.

The army's top commander, General William T. Sherman, who was on an inspection tour of the West, left Yellowstone Park as the Nez Percés approached. Letters he wrote to the secretary of war in Washington, D.C., during this tour show that Sherman and the government had known that the retreating bands were peaceful before the bloody fight at Big Hole Valley. But, Sherman wrote, all these people should be "punished," not only for the murders back in Idaho but also for "going to war without any just cause or provocation. . . . I hope hourly," Sherman reported, "to hear that [Howard] has finished up what General Gibbon so well began."

But the Nez Percé warriors did not give Howard the chance. Early on the morning of August 20 they returned with Ollokot and Looking Glass to Camas Meadows, where Howard and his men had camped. Attacking at dawn, the men made off with nearly all of Howard's mules and fought off frantic attempts to recover them. The bands did not move, getting their first day of rest since Big Hole. The chase resumed the next day, but on August 23, Howard's pursuit collapsed due to the exhaustion of his men and remaining horses. The bands disappeared, driving Howard's mules into the forested mountains of Yellowstone Park as the general pulled back to refit.

In their repeated defeats of the army and their brave march across the country, the nontreaty band had by now created a national sensation. Part of the nation's white population began to feel sympathy for people who were fighting courageously for their freedom and who had not killed women and children nor mutilated the dead in the war.

Sherman sent fresh troops to block exits from the north, east and south of Yellowstone Park. But Joseph and the Nez Percés had vanished. From August 23 to September 8, their scouts scattered in a thin but deadly cloud that blinded the enemy. Army officers sent their own scouts in and persuaded miners to spy, only to find their bodies later. To the Nez Percés, every white man was now an enemy to be either killed or captured.

Frank Carpenter was one of the lucky ones who lived. He had come to Yellowstone with a party of friends, including two of his sisters, to see the hot springs and the geysers near the western side of the park, right near the route that Poker Joe chose for his people. Yellow Wolf and two others captured Carpenter and his party on the morning of August 24. Carpenter later described the retreating bands. "As far as we could see, up and down the river, they were moving abreast in an unbroken line 10 or 15 feet deep, driving ponies and constantly riding out and in the line. We could see about three miles of Indians, with one thousand or 1500 ponies."

Angry warriors tried to kill several of the men in Carpenter's group and wounded one badly before he escaped. That night Joseph had Carpenter and Emma Cowan, Carpenter's sister, stay at his campfire for safety. "My brother tried to converse with Chief Joseph," Emma Cowan recalled, "but without avail. The chief sat by the fire, somber and silent . . . Grave and dignified, he looked a chief. A squaw sat down near me with a babe in her arms. My brother, wishing to conciliate them, I suppose, lifted it up and placed it in my lap . . . It stared at me with big black eyes . . . I glanced at the chief and saw a glimmer of a smile on his face . . ."

That night by Joseph's fire the only food was a mush of camas root. Hard days of travel still lay ahead, and the horses were very thin and worn. The bands passed north of Yellowstone lake and entered the forbidding, thickly forested Absoraka Mountains, avoiding better traveled routes where they knew the soldiers would be. The trail was thick with fallen timber. Howard's scouts found it littered with dead and lame horses.

East of the park, Colonel Samuel D. Sturgis and men of the 7th Cavalry waited by Clarks Fork River (not the same Clarks Fork that flows to the Columbia River), which flows southeast from the Absoraka Mountains and then twists north into the plains. Unless the Nez Percés headed north where other troops waited or went far out of their way to the south, Clarks Fork offered the only pathway out of the nearly impassable mountains.

Sturgis, cut off by the warriors from Howard's dispatches about the movements of the band, waited and searched nervously for an invisible foe. On September 6 he was lured to the south, either by his own ignorance or a ruse by the Nez Percés, and the bands moved east from the mountains and passed his army.

They pressed on down the Clarks Fork to the Yellowstone River, their horses spent and their food all but gone. By now Looking Glass had made contact with some of his friends among the Crow bands, who had told him that the army would press the Crows to fight the Nez Percés. Some would fight half-heartedly, some would give in to the urge to go after horses. The Nez Percé bands could not rest with the Crows; they must run to Canada. They crossed the Yellowstone and were traveling toward the ravine of Canyon Creek to get to the plains above the river on September 13. Then Sturgis caught them. Having driven his men and horses almost to exhaustion he now moved across the rocky ground, becoming the fifth army officer to lead an attack on the embattled bands. They held him back, posting men in the bluffs above the ravine to check a cavalry charge. The bands escaped up the creek and Sturgis's advance, like Howard's before it, collapsed. Howard and Sturgis toiled slowly after their retreating foe, losing ground each day.

The September nights on the prairie were cool, and the people had no tipis. They had captured some food in raids near the Yellowstone and they may have eaten some horse meat, but they also went hungry. On the 23rd of September, 10 days after the battle at Canyon Creek, they finally reached the Missouri River and raided an army depot loaded with food and supplies. They moved north from the river, more slowly now, resting and grazing their starved horses as the scouts watched the country behind them for the enemy and the country ahead for buffalo.

Joseph remembered,

Several days passed, and we heard nothing of generals Howard, or Gibbon, or Sturgis. We had repulsed each in turn, and began to feel secure. . . . I sat down in a fat and beautiful country. I had won my freedom and the freedom of my people. There were many empty places in the lodges and in the council, but we were in the land where we would not be forced to live in a place we did not want. I believed that if I could remain safe at a distance and talk straight to the men that would be sent by the Great Father I could get back to the Wallowa Valley and return in peace.

So far the Nez Percés had prevailed. When the war moved into the Great Plains, the government enlisted a powerful ally, the steam engine. Steam boats and locomotives mobilized fresh men and supplies for yet another assault.

The man behind this latest attack, Colonel Nelson Miles, was a master of logistics who had managed to keep his troops in the field throughout the previous winter in the war against the Sioux. An ambitious man, Miles had learned to respect Native American fighters. He assembled a crack force of 400 troops and Cheyenne scouts, and they moved quickly north and west from the Missouri River.

Miles closed in on the bands as they camped along Snake Creek 40 miles south of Canada, in a gap between the Bear Paws Mountains. The scouts were able to give the people little warning. Yellow Wolf was with Joseph when the warning came.

A wild stir hit the people. Great hurrying everywhere. I was still in my uncle's camp, my home. I saw this uncle, Chief Joseph, leap to the open. His voice was above all the noise as he called, "Horses! Horses! Save the horses!" I grabbed my rifle and cartridge belts and ran with others for our horses. Warriors were hurrying to the bluffs to meet the soldiers. Soon, from the south came a noise—a rumble like stampeding buffaloes. Reaching the higher ground north of our camp I looked back. Hundreds of soldiers charging in two wide, circling wings. They were surrounding our camp.

Joseph, his daughter Khap-khap-onmi and Yellow Wolf ran with dozens of other people to bring the horses into camp where the people could mount and escape. But it was too late. One of the charging wings drove the horses away and closed around the camp. "About 70 men, myself among them, were cut off," Joseph said.

> My little daughter, twelve years of age, was with me. I gave her a rope, and told her to catch a horse and join the others who were cut off from the camp. . . .
> I thought of my wife and children, who were now surrounded by soldiers, and resolved to go to them or die. With a prayer in my mouth to the Creator, I dashed unarmed through the line of soldiers. It seemed to me that there were guns on every side, before and behind me. My clothes were cut to pieces and my horse was wounded, but I was not hurt. As I reached the door of my lodge, my wife handed me a rifle, saying: "Here's your gun. Fight!"

Joseph soon learned that he must now lead the Wallowa fighters. Ollokot was dead. Khap-khap-onmi fled north toward Canada with most of the other people cut off in the charge. Yellow Wolf returned and waited for dark to sneak past the soldiers and reach his people.

> A long time I watched. It was snowing. The wind was cold! Stripped for battle, I had no blanket. I lay close to the ground crawling nearer the guard line. It was past middle of night when I went between those guards. . . . on the bluffs Indians with knives were digging rifle pits. Some had those broad-bladed knives taken from soldiers at the Big Hole. Down in the main camp women with camas hooks were digging shelter pits . . . You have seen hail, sometimes, leveling the grass. Indians were so leveled by the bullet hail. Most of our few warriors left from the Big Hole had been swept as leaves before the storm. Chief Ollokot, Lone Bird and Lean Elk [Poker Joe] were gone . . .
> I looked around. Some were burying their dead. A young warrior, wounded, lay on a buffalo robe, dying without complaint. Children crying with cold. No fire, there could be no light. Everywhere the crying, the death wail. My heart became fire. I joined the warriors digging rifle pits. All the rest of night we worked.
> Morning came, bringing the battle anew. Bullets from everywhere! A big gun throwing bursting shells. From rifle pits, warriors returned shot for shot. Wild and stormy, the cold wind was thick with snow. Air filled with smoke of

powder. Flash of guns through it all . . . I felt the approaching end.

For five bleak and bitter days, the Nez Percés struggled. "The fight was a very severe and desperate one," Miles wrote to his wife, "as they were caught and of course fought for their lives. Our loss was very great . . ."

On the sixth day, as Howard arrived with his Nez Percé scouts, Miles sent them up to appeal for an end to the fighting. In a council after the scouts left, Joseph said he would surrender in return for a promise that the bands could go back to the reservation in Idaho. Looking Glass opposed him, but Joseph was unswayed.

> I could not bear to see my wounded men and women suffer any longer; we had lost enough already. General Miles had promised that we might return to our country with what stock we had left. I thought we could start again. I believed General Miles or I never would have surrendered . . .

A short time later, while looking to the north in hopes of seeing the Sioux riding to their rescue, Looking Glass was hit by a shot and killed. When Howard's scouts returned for his answer Joseph said,

> Tell General Howard I know his heart. What he has told me I have in my heart. I am tired of fighting. Our chiefs are killed. Looking Glass is dead. Toolhoolhoolzote is dead. The old men are all dead. It is the young men who say yes or no. He who leads the young men [Ollokot] is dead. It is cold and we have no blankets. The little children are freezing to death. My people, some of them, have run away to the hills and have no blankets, no food; no one knows where they are—maybe freezing to death. I want time to look for my children and see how many of them I can find. Maybe I shall find them among the dead. Hear me my chiefs. I am tired. My heart is sick and sad. From where the sun now stands I will fight no more forever.

A reporter recorded the scene as Joseph gave up his gun:

> As the sun was dropping to the level of the prairie and tingling the tawny and white land with waves of ruddy

light, Joseph came slowly riding up the hill. Five of his followers walked beside him; he, the only one on horseback, in the center of the group. His hands were crossed on the pommel of the saddle, his head bowed upon his breast. His warriors talked in eager murmurs, he listening and making no reply.

As evening fell, scores of Nez Percés sneaked northward from the battlefield rather than go to Miles. Like those who had escaped the fighting earlier, they headed for Canada and the camp of Sitting Bull. Some made, it, some froze on the plains or were killed by bands from other tribes who Miles had earlier encouraged to attack the Nez Percés. All told, Miles had 431 captives as he marched southeast from the battlefield. One hundred to 150 had escaped, including Yellow Wolf and Joseph's daughter, Khap-khap-onmi. About the same number died in the war. Some of the escapees would be captured later.

Miles planned to hold the Nez Percés at Fort Keogh, near the mouth of the Yellowstone River, for the winter and then send them to the Idaho reservation, as he had promised Joseph. But a week after reaching the fort, Miles received orders from Sherman to ship the prisoners 800 miles down the Missouri

Bear Paws, Montana, the last battlefield of the war of 1877, where the Nez Percés defended themselves for five days at Snake Creek before Chief Joseph made the agonizing decision to surrender. (Courtesy Historical Photograph Collections, Washington State University)

River to Fort Lincoln, in the Dakota Territory. Joseph protested in vain. Miles hired flatboats to carry women, children, elderly and wounded while he traveled with the remaining men on horseback. It was late November, and by the time the boats and columns of men reached Fort Lincoln, ice had begun to clog the rivers.

Across the river from the fort, in the town of Bismarck, Fred Bond, one of the boatmen who had carried the prisoners down the river, watched as Miles and Joseph led warriors and troops into town. "The band was playing the Star Spangled Banner," the boatman later wrote.

> Gen. Miles with Chief Joseph on his left was in the advance. The appearance of all was heart-rending, very sad. At the corner of Main and 4th Street the stampede commenced. Women, children and even men rushed . . . with all kinds of cooked food . . . The command had to halt till each Nez Percés prisoner and even the over land guard was furnished with food of good kind. The officers of the command said nothing till all was given and it was a wise movement on their part for there stood nearby fully 300 armed determined men.

The townspeople, who had heard stories of the struggle of the Nez Percés and felt sympathy, gave Joseph salmon at a dinner in his honor. By then new orders had come for Miles to ship them off for confinement at Fort Leavenworth in Kansas. Joseph spoke to his hosts of goodwill but was sick from grief and worry.

> Just as you plant a good tree to grow good fruit, I keep good sentiments to make a good man . . . I expect what I speak will be said throughout the land and I only want to speak good.

But at this point, a reporter wrote, Joseph seemed overcome, and could say no more.

The next day, Bond recalled,

> . . . Chief Joseph stood on the rear platform of the train to wave goodbye. Just before the train started the Belle of Bismarck kissed the chief on the cheek a goodbye for all the people of the Northwest.

9

IN EIKISH PAH
A Fight for Life
December 1877–85

The train steamed slowly east from Bismarck, across the rolling plains of North Dakota, into the lake country of northern Minnesota and on through the flatlands of Nebraska and Iowa. For four days the people, including 147 children, lay under guard on the train. They "were much crowded in their cars, and their thirst was merely mocked by the tin reservoir in the car ends," one of the trainmen remembered. "So stops were made at water tanks where the Indians filed out and drank by the bucketfull."

The Nez Percés had heard of the machine with the power of many horses that belched smoke and steam. This locomotive, the first one they saw, hauled them away from the last of their horses and far, far away from the northern plains, the Rockies and the Northwest. The people lost about 100 fine saddles along with their horses. They had with them their tipis and their remaining household goods, packed into freight cars and a few treasured personal things.

At one station where the train stopped for food, the officers invited Joseph to their private car for supper. Afterward he got away from the train somehow and it left without him. Guards soon realized that the chief was missing, the trainman said, and a "thorough search was made through the train—but unsuccessfully. This was a loss not to be overlooked ... and the train was slowly backed up." They soon found him, running toward them along the track. "In one corner of his blanket he was carrying something which proved to be pies, rather dilapidated, but food for the sick squaws—as Joseph explained."

The train stopped for the last time at Fort Leavenworth, a few miles upstream from Independence, Missouri, the old gateway to the Oregon Trail. Here, on the orders of army commander William T. Sherman, the captive Nez Percés began eight years of confinement, death and torment. The bands had faced six army officers in war: Perry, Parnell, Howard, Gibbon, Sturgis and Miles. In defeat they faced Sherman, who took a heavier toll than the other six officers combined.

Sherman, with Howard at his side, had driven an army through the Confederacy. He was the tough hero who crushed slavery by burning and razing the southern heartland. This was mild compared to his treatment of Native Americans after the Civil War, when he became commander of the army and directed campaigns against the Native Americans. Officers, like Custer, who targeted women and children as well as warriors did so on the personal authorization of Sherman.

As the Nez Percés traveled into captivity, the general saluted them in his report to Congress. They had "displayed a courage and skill that elicited universal praise," he wrote. "They abstained from scalping, let captive women go free, did not commit indiscriminate murder of peaceful families, which is usual, and fought with almost scientific skill, using advance and rear guards, skirmish lines and field fortifications." But Sherman rejected a proposal to punish the handful of surviving Nez Percé braves who had stained their hands in the Salmon River raids. Instead, he insisted on punishing all the people "as a tribe." He recommended that the Nez Percé bands "never return" to the Northwest; he sent them all into exile where the innocent, both the old and young, sickened and died.

General John B. Pope, army commander in Kansas, received the Nez Percé prisoners at Leavenworth on November 27. He asked permission to move them 100 miles west to Fort Riley, where, he wrote, he could provide reasonably healthy conditions for more than 400 people. Sherman overruled him and ordered the prisoners held at Leavenworth, where the army had nothing for them—not even a supply of clean water.

The prisoners ended up in a camp on a spit of land upstream from the fort, between the polluted Missouri River and a stagnant lagoon. Joseph said:

We were placed on a low river bottom, with no water except river water to drink and cook with. We had always lived in a healthy country, where the mountains were high and the water was cold and clear. Many of our people sickened and died, and we buried them in this strange land. I cannot tell how much my heart suffered for the people while at Leavenworth. The One who rules above seemed to be looking the other way and did not see what was being done.

A writer who visited the bands a few months later was appalled at what he saw. The conditions reminded him of a Civil War prison camp whose Confederate commandant, Henry Wirz, had been convicted of war crimes and executed for allowing his Union prisoners to die of starvation, disease and neglect. The people, he wrote, "presented a picture which brought to my mind the horrors of Andersonville. One half were sick, principally women and children. . . .They had better be moved soon or their removal to the burial ground will be completed." Joseph persuaded the commandant at Leavenworth to send a petition to Sherman calling on the general to send the bands home to Idaho or to at least let them find a healthier place to live. Sherman did not answer, except to reprimand the commandant for sending the petition.

Instead of bullets the people faced malaria, caused by a parasite carried by mosquitoes. It gradually weakens its victims in bouts of intense fever, chills and shaking. As the cold and damp of winter gave way to the spring of 1878, heat intensified the suffering, and the death toll climbed. Defeated in war, racked by disease and convinced they would never see their homeland again, the people fell into despair. Loss of faith in spiritual power and traditional medicine quickened the pace of death.

Spring gave way to a torrid summer, as the army handed the captives over to the Department of the Interior. Word of the transfer came "during the hot days," as Joseph put it, in July 1878. "We were ordered to get into the railroad cars." The train rolled south across Kansas to Baxter Springs, just north of Indian Territory, the present-day state of Oklahoma. The United States had established the territory as a huge Indian reserve decades before and had exiled tribes to this territory from all over the nation.

Joseph felt bitter remorse over his decision to surrender. "Three of my people died on the way to Baxter Springs," he said. "It was worse to die there than to die fighting in the mountains." Though Sherman had yielded formal control, the government continued to push the people toward the fate he had decreed.

From Baxter Springs the people were loaded into wagons and hauled 25 miles south into Indian Territory, to the edge of a small allotment on the Quapaw reservation. Here the government had sent the remnants of the Modoc people from southern Oregon after the army had crushed them in 1874. The reservation agent did not provide wagons for the Nez Percé tipis, which had to be left behind at Baxter Springs. Food was scanty and poor. The bands, Joseph said, were "set down without our lodges. We had but little medicine and we were nearly all sick."

The small band of Modocs tried to help, bringing fresh produce to the Nez Percés to welcome them with a feast. But they could do little for so many, and rain poured down upon the sick people. By the end of 1878, many dozens more lay in their graves.

Joseph was able to communicate with his daughter Khap-khap-onmi, who with Yellow Wolf stayed among Sitting Bull's Sioux in Canada. Joseph sent her a copy of the picture that had been made of him in Bismarck. In the summer of 1878 Yellow Wolf took her and a small band of other Nez Percés into the United States and through many perils back to the reservation in Idaho. Khap-khap-onmi was allowed to stay there. Monteith sent Yellow Wolf to Joseph in the Indian Territory.

At the Quapaw reserve "the climate killed many of us," Yellow Wolf said. "All the newborn babies died, and many of the old people too . . . We called where we were held Eikish Pah (Hot Place). All the time, night and day, we suffered from the climate." The girl who had been born to Joseph and Toma Alwawinmi in 1877 died. Toma Alwawinmi also died, in the war or in exile.

Joseph returned to his prewar role of tirelessly advocating his people's cause. He kept doggedly at it, searching for a path to survival as years passed and graves accumulated, and as he fell into despair. Whether consciously or not, Joseph exploited the fame he had achieved as an advocate for his people and, false though it was, as a military genius. As sympathizers circulated the news about what was happening, senators and Interior Department officials found it difficult to ignore the situation. The public had learned about the Nez Percés during the war and, as the citizens of Bismarck had shown, many felt sympathy for the embattled bands. Interior Department officials, congressmen, even Leonard F. Grover, the former Oregon governor and now a U.S. senator, set off for Indian Territory to show their concern. There they witnessed what was happening, and Joseph confronted them personally.

Something about him inspired deep reverence in many of the people who met him in those years. Nelson Miles, whose ambition drove him to claim credit for Joseph's capture, acted much differently after he had ridden the trail from Bear Paws to Bismarck with the chief. Years after the war was over, while the tribe still languished in Indian Territory and his own career prospered, Miles penned appeals for the bands and met with Joseph in an effort to call attention to his cause. Joseph kept the pressure on Miles, reminding the general of the promises he had sealed with his word at Bear Paws.

E. A. Hayt, the commissioner of Indian affairs, came to the territory late in 1878 after Joseph blocked a move to deed worthless land at Quapaw to the bands. The chief told him, he reported, "that the land selected for him on the Quapaw Reservation was not fertile, and that water was exceedingly scarce on it; that two wells had been dug to a depth of 60 to 70 feet without reaching water; and that he did not like the country. He thought it unhealthy, and a very hard place for an Indian to earn his living by tilling the soil."

Hayt traveled several days on horseback with Joseph seeking better land. They went more than 100 miles west, to the Ponca reserve south of Arkansas City. There, while still insisting on the government's obligation to return the people to the Northwest, Joseph agreed to accept land.

"I like the land we found better than any place in that country; but it is not a healthy land," Joseph said. "I promised Chief Hayt to go there, and do the best I could until the Government got ready to make good General Miles' word. I was not satisfied but I could not help myself."

Early in 1879, while the people waited for spring and the move to Ponca, Miles and other supporters won permission for Joseph to come to Washington, D.C., to make his case personally for the return of the bands to Idaho. He made the journey with Yellow Bull and with Chapman who knew the Nez Percé language and had become an interpreter for the government. Joseph told his story in a series of meetings and interviews.

At the end of his story, Joseph would call for the government to honor the battlefield agreement with Miles, to send his people to the Idaho reservation or at least to send them somewhere "where they will not die so fast." He was heartsick and exasperated.

> I have seen the Great Father Chief [president]; the next Great Chief [interior secretary]; the Law Chief [attorney general] and many other law chiefs [congressmen] and they all say they are my friends and that I shall have justice, but while their mouths talk right I do not understand why nothing is done for my people. I have heard talk and talk, but nothing is done . . . Good words will not give me back my children. . . . Good words will not get my people a home where they can live in peace and take care of themselves. I am tired of talk that comes to nothing. It makes my heart sick when I remember all the good words and all the broken promises.

While he was in Washington word reached Joseph that three more of his people had died. Though he was desperate to get the bands out of Indian Territory, Joseph boldly attacked the unequal justice and racism of the government whose help he so urgently needed.

> If the white man wants to live in peace with the Indian he can live in peace. There need be no trouble. Treat all men alike. Give them all the same law. Give them all an even chance to live and grow. All men were made by the same Creator. They are all brothers. The earth is the mother of all people, and all people should have equal rights upon it. You might as well expect the rivers to run backward as that any man who was born a free man should be contented penned up and denied liberty to go where he pleases. If you tie a horse to a stake, do you expect he will grow fat? . . . I have asked some of the great white chiefs where they get their authority to say to the Indian that he shall stay in one place, while he sees white men going where they please. They cannot tell me . . .
>
> When I think of our condition my heart is heavy. I see men of my race treated as outlaws and driven from country to country, or shot down like animals.

I know that my race must change. We cannot hold our own with the white men as we are. We only ask an even chance to live as other men live. We ask to be recognized as men. We ask that the same law shall work alike on all men. If the Indian breaks the law, punish him by that law. If the white man breaks the law, punish him also.

Let me be a free man—free to travel, free to stop, free to work, free to trade, where I choose, free to choose my own teachers, free to follow the religion of my fathers, free to think and talk and act for myself—and I will obey every law, or submit to the penalty.

. . . We shall all be alike—brothers of one father and one mother, with one sky above us and one country around us, and one government for all. Then the One who rules above will smile upon this land, and send rain to wash out the bloody spots made by brothers' hands upon the face of the earth. For this time the Indian race are waiting and praying. I hope that no more groans of wounded men and women will ever go to the ear of the One above, and that all people may be one people.

This statement would have been impressive in any context, but, coming in the midst of calamity, it shows extraordinary courage and determination. Joseph could see the white people taking his words down. It was a rare opportunity to speak out to all people and to the future. Joseph used it to leave a testament for human rights.

Joseph's speeches in Washington helped undermine the government's policy of sending tribes to exile in the Indian Territory; they won broader sympathy for his cause. But they did not end the agony of the captives in Eikish Pah.

They took to the wagons in the summer of 1879 for the seven-day trek to the Ponca reserve. Again no provision was made at the new location for food, shelter or medicine. As he buried more of his people, Joseph sank ever deeper into despair. When a former Indian Affairs official who still supported the Indian Territory settlement policy came to him that summer, Joseph was blunt and bitter:

You come to see me as you would a man upon his death bed. The One above has left me and my people to our fate. The white men forget us, and death comes almost every day for some of my people. He will come for all of us. A few

months more and we will be in the ground. We are a
doomed people.

Some of the people turned to Christianity. A few, at least
three, committed suicide. Joseph kept doggedly on, appealing
to every agent, every army officer, congressman or petty official
who came within reach. One after another, they wrote to
Washington, D.C., that the Nez Percés should be sent home.
"No other tribe moved to this territory has a better claim to
be returned to its homeland," an army officer wrote in 1879. "A
great wrong has been done this people." Letters like this came
year after year.

The death rate began a slow decline at Ponca, probably
because the people had some chance to help themselves and
because they had already lost so many of the weaker ones, the
children and elderly. But the diseases they had picked up
earlier persisted. The government gave the bands 100 head of
cattle in 1880, and the agent marveled at their ability as
herders. The people, including Joseph, began to have some
success at growing food. The land was not as barren as
Quapaw. But white cattlemen took their pasture and stole
their stock.

As a national movement began to demand the return of the
bands to the Northwest, some officials in Washington, particularly those who had met Joseph, lent support.

In 1881 Miles renewed his efforts to fulfill his promise to
Joseph at Bear Paws. He appealed publicly to President Ruth-
erford Hayes, putting him on the spot. The president ordered
an investigation. The following year the commissioner of Indian Affairs recommended returning the bands to Idaho. A
succession of agents came and went at the Ponca reserve, and
each one added his voice to the chorus. In 1883 the Interior
Department allowed 29 widows and orphans to move to the
reservation in Idaho. The following year, in the spring, the
return of the remaining people became a national issue. Peti-
tions poured into Congress, one of them circulated by President
James Garfield's wife. Congress soon passed and the president
signed legislation authorizing the Interior Department to send
the bands west.

Another year passed before the department decided what to
do. Monteith did not want Joseph on the reservation, and

WAR AND CAPTIVITY TRAILS

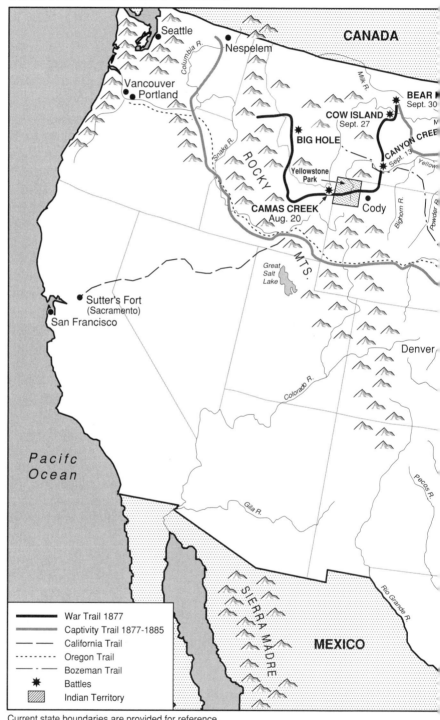

Seattle
Nespelem
CANADA

Vancouver
Portland

Columbia R.
Milk R.

ROCKY

Snake R.

BEAR
Sept. 30

COW ISLAND
(Sept. 27)

M

CANYON CREE
Sept. 13

Yellow

BIG HOLE

Yellowstone
Park

Cody

Bighorn R.

Powder R.

CAMAS CREEK
Aug. 20

Great
Salt
Lake

MTS.

Sutter's Fort
(Sacramento)
San Francisco

Denver

Colorado R.

Pacifc
Ocean

Gila R.

Pecos R.

SIERRA MADRE

Rio Grande R.

MEXICO

▬▬▬	War Trail 1877
▬▬▬	Captivity Trail 1877-1885
— —	California Trail
··········	Oregon Trail
—·—·—	Bozeman Trail
✳	Battles
▨	Indian Territory

Current state boundaries are provided for reference.

officials in Idaho wanted to try him on trumped up murder charges. Finally the department decided to send Joseph to the Colville reservation in northeastern Washington with any other Nez Percés considered likely to resist "civilization." Monteith would take the rest.

The Interior Department gave Miles permission to take personal charged of the transfer. He sent a doctor, W. H. Faulkner, to help the Nez Percés sell off their stock and land and to accompany them on the journey. In mid-May 1885, as the hot days began again, a line of wagons pulled away from Ponca and headed for Arkansas City and the railroad, two days journey north. As they left, the 268 people who had survived Sherman's revenge took a mournful parting from the dead they left behind at Leavenworth, Quapaw and Ponca.

The captive Nez Percés had begun their exile with nearly 150 children. They emerged almost eight years later with no more than 40—including the orphans who went home in 1883—plus 30 babies who were born in the Hot Place and survived long enough to leave. Of the 100 or more children missing in 1885, a few may have grown to adulthood in exile. But the weight of evidence from accounts by the Nez Percés and by outside observers is that the great majority perished. The mortality rate among adults was roughly one in three, or about 100 people, with many of the victims being elderly.

For Joseph, for any chief, for any man or woman, protection of children is the most sacred duty. We can only guess about how they felt as they rolled west with their remaining children. Many were broken down and broken hearted. But they had escaped the fate decreed by Sherman and returned to the Northwest. They brought with them the story of their struggle, to be remembered and passed on among the native peoples of the Northwest.

The train paused at Pocatello in eastern Idaho, then pressed on after an army officer warned Faulkner that a sheriff was on his way there to arrest Joseph and several other men. While the rest of the country had been taught the myth of Joseph as a brave and determined general, northern Idaho Indian-haters had spread the myth of Joseph as a bloodthirsty villain who had led the Salmon River raiders and murdered a defenseless woman with his own hands. He had been indicted for murder.

They rolled on across southern Idaho, now with soldiers for protection. The railroad track, built while the Nez Percés were in exile, followed the Oregon Trail along the Snake River. It turned west above Hell's Canyon and cut across the northeast corner of Oregon near the Wallowa Mountains. The train climbed through the Blue Mountains and, near the end of May, reached the Columbia River and Wallula Junction at the mouth of the Walla Walla River in Washington.

There, according to Yellow Wolf, the white authorities sorted the people out with a simple question: "Do you want to go to Idaho and be a Christian or go to Colville and just be yourself?" Monteith took 148 of the Nez Percés to join relatives in Idaho. He wrote that it was proper "to make a distinction between the subdued and the unsubdued" and that the people he took to Lapwaii were "very much broken in spirit" and would provide sobering examples "for the more restless members of the tribe who are not disposed to settle down and enter upon civilized pursuits."

Joseph and 109 others, including most of the surviving Wallowa people, stayed several days at Fort Walla Walla as they waited for a train to take them to the Colville reservation. A local boy who went to the swimming hole in back of the fort saw them, bathing in the cool water of a Northwest mountain river for the first time in eight long years. He stared at the large, muscular men with the long, ragged scars on their bodies.

10
LET MY PEOPLE GO
A Fight for the Future 1885–1904

After traveling there by train and wagon, Joseph and his band spent the rest of 1885 at Fort Spokane on the northeastern edge of the Columbia Plain, and moved to the Nespelem Valley on the Colville reservation at the end of the year. The Colville reserve was a large, mountainous region isolated by the wide Columbia River on the east and south, the Cascade Mountains to the west and the Canadian border to the north. It had been established in 1872 for tribes of the northern Columbia Plain region who lost their lands. Some of these groups were not happy about having to make room for another band, especially one that had no traditional claim to the country. The Nez Percé band did not formally receive approval to live at Nespelem until mid-1887.

The Nespelem River flows south between mountain ridges to the Columbia. The country is not as lush as the Wallowa, but the Nez Percés found it quite an improvement over the Indian Territory. "On the Colville [reserve] we found wild game aplenty," Yellow Wolf said, "fish, berries, and all kinds of roots . . . It was better than Idaho, where all Christian Nez Percés and whites were against us." But fish, game and wild plants had always been seasonal food sources, and the Nez Percés could not get enough at Colville to last through the year. They did not have the livestock or the pasture needed to resume raising cattle for food or horses for trading. Hunting, gathering and herding remained important and allowed them to continue traditional patterns of life. But these pursuits could not sustain life. The Nez Percés at Colville depended partly on rations from the government that had expelled them from their home and still held them in exile as prisoners of war.

Chief Joseph's summer camp at Nespelem, Washington. (Courtesy Smithsonian Institution, BAE Collection. Neg. 2987.B-4)

Joseph's first wife, Hy-yum-yu-yik-ty, left the band and went back to the reservation in Idaho to stay with her people in Kamiah. He married two more women, both of whom had been widowed in the war: Iatowenonmy, born 1866, who had been married to Looking Glass; and Wawintepiksat, born 1855, whose first husband had also died at Bear Paws. Two or more children—either adopted or born in the previous marriages of his wives—were part of the household at various times.

Joseph had no child born after 1877. There is evidence that Joseph's last surviving child Khap-khap-onmi, who had settled on the Idaho reservation, came to Nespelem to stay with her father. She had married in 1879 and had children, but none survived. She herself died, probably before 1890 and certainly by 1900, leaving Joseph with no descendants.

As most of Joseph's people were forced toward the life of landless and land-poor laborers, Joseph upheld the life and customs, the values and ideals of the society they had come from. He fought unceasingly against the government's attempts to root out every fragment of native cultures—to sever their traditional bonds to the land, extinguish their languages, take control of their young and eradicate all signs of native life right down to the hair styles. He became a symbol of freedom to many Nez Percés on the reservation in Idaho and among tribes across the Northwest.

In the late 1880s the government began its "assimilation" policy, which superseded the practice of establishing reservations. Rather than allow tribes to keep legal title to their reserves, to exclude whites and to continue some aspects of tribal government, the U.S. government decided it would be better to chop the reservations up into parcels and let each Native American family have a deed for its own land, the same as white Americans. These parcels would be so small that only a fraction of the land in the country's reservations would be needed to create them. The rest of the reservation lands would be declared "surplus" and sold to whites. Thus, Native Americans would be "assimilated" by becoming neighbors of white people and part of the same economy. They would become farmers and their children would go to schools that would teach them to be like white people.

"Assimilation" was an overall strategy for eliminating Native American culture. The Allotment Act of 1887 was the instrument for dismembering the reservations. It authorized the government to send agents out to survey the lands, draw up deeds for the Native Americans' portions and dispose of the "surplus" land. The program was initiated at the Idaho reservation in 1889.

In 1890, the government invited Joseph's people to move from the Colville reservation in Washington to the Nez Percé reservation in Idaho and take land there under the Allotment Act. Yellow Bull, who was from Idaho, and about a dozen of his people accepted the proposal. Joseph traveled to the Kamiah area to meet the allotment agent, anthropologist Alice Fletcher, and her assistant Elizabeth Gay. The chief told them that he and his people would accept allotment—but only in their own home, the Wallowa country. "He cannot be persuaded to take his land upon the [Idaho] reservation," Gay wrote. "He will have none but the Wallowa valley . . . It was good to see an unsubjugated Indian. One could not help respecting the man who still stood firmly for his rights . . ." Gay could do nothing about land in the Wallowa country, so Joseph and his people stayed at Nespelem. Allotment did not come to Colville until after Joseph's death.

On his visit to Idaho, Joseph led the annual 4th of July parade in which hundreds of the People dressed in traditional attire and rode several miles along Lapwaii Creek, singing, reciting stories of the war and mourning for the dead. Joseph returned to lead at least one more of these processions. The reservation agents at first considered them harmless pageantry. "If the white people only knew how we feel," one man confided to Gay "if they only knew what these songs mean to us, there would be no more" parades. Later the agents caught on and banned the parades. Joseph continued to lead parades at Nespelem.

A 13-year-old boy, Erskine Wood, witnessed the Nez Percé life at Nespelem when he came there to live with Joseph. His father, Colonel Charles E. S. Wood, had fought the Nez Percés under Howard and befriended Joseph after the surrender. The two men resumed contact after Joseph reached Nespelem, when Wood was living in Portland. Wishing his son to experience the Nez Percé way of life, Wood sent his son to spend the late summer and fall with Joseph in 1892 and again the following year, a total of eight months. Years later, when he was old, Erskine Wood had vivid memories of the chief he had come to revere. Joseph, he wrote,

> lived quietly near the Agency in the little Nespelem Valley, Washington, with his two wives, and shared his tipi with another family . . . He was the kindest of fathers to me . . . Joseph was well built, slightly heavy set, maybe a little overweight, dignified as a Roman senator, with a forelock and two long braids of black hair. Usually he wore a dark blue flannel shirt, breechcloth, blanket leggings and buckskin moccasins.
>
> I have often been asked about Joseph's two wives . . . Well, I was only a small boy. I wasn't interested in that. All I know is that they lived in perfect harmony together, the wives uniting in the household life, and that they all three slept together. In what order or by what arrangement, I do not know. I was not interested. My strong recollection is that Joseph slept in the middle between the two women.

Sometimes Wood saw Joseph staring off into space, but the chief did not seem sad to him. "He enjoyed his family and the company of his men friends. He used to have them in for breakfast on Sundays or other occasions, or they would gather in his tipi in the evenings to pass the pipe around the fire. He

Chief Joseph's winter camp at Nespelem, Washington. Joseph, his wives and their adopted children often shared a compound tipi with another family during winter. (Courtesy Special Collections Division, University of Washington Libraries, Negative UW 12355)

enjoyed the horse races. He enjoyed the hunt, and the general Indian life that was left to him . . ."

One hundred or more Nez Percés in the band lived in the valley. Most stayed in tipis, raised livestock and observed the traditional form of self government around the campfire of their chief. "Joseph's leadership was never questioned," Erskine wrote. "Many of the band consulted him. When a need for decisions arose, such as how to divide venison, all others stood back while Joseph cut into the deer." Joseph did not drink, gamble or bet on horses. But, Wood wrote, he always presided over the races, when the people dressed up and rode to the competition on the flat ground by the Nespelem.

They camped at different spots in the valley and scattered into the mountains for the fall hunt. In winter they camped near the agency in Nespelem, where they received rations.

Erskine and Joseph's adopted son, Mickey Cowlitz, spent much of their time fishing, hunting small game and caring for the 50 horses the chief owned. In the fall, when the band scattered and moved into the mountains, Joseph took Erskine along on deer hunts. In a diary he kept, the boy described the cooperative methods Nez Percé men used to spread out and comb an area for game without losing track of each other.

By the end of his second stay, in 1893, the white boy revered the Nez Percé chief. "His voice was melodious. Of course I never mastered the language to follow it or speak it fluently, but I know that his voice was rich and his words eloquent. I think this was especially noticeable when he offered prayers before Sunday morning breakfast."

Another young observer, teenager Frances Hamblen, also felt Joseph's ability to communicate across the language barrier when he visited her father in Spokane that summer of 1893. "Joseph does not speak good English," she wrote,

[He] mixes in a number of Nez Percés words, but it is almost possible to understand him by his gestures, without any words. In these he is perfectly free and unconscious, moving with a native grace that is very pleasing. . . . We asked him if he had hunted lately. Yes he killed a hi-u (big) grizzly this winter. He measured the height the bear stood from the floor. . . .

He told us how he lived away from his people—how his wife had died, his children, all his family and putting his hand on his heart, he shook his head, "sick-sick."

I asked him to tell me his Indian name—he merely grunted and shook his head. I asked again and he must have concluded I was in earnest, for suddenly he leaned towards me in his chair and told his name, waiting for me to repeat each syllable after him. "Hin-mah-too-ya-lat-kekht," the last syllable in true Indian style between a cough and a spit. When we had done this together several times, he told us what it meant, . . . "Thunder in mountains," and with his arm he described the course of the thunder which reached from the base to the very summit of the mountains. His voice, too, was rich and full . . ."

Late that December of 1893, Joseph and Erskine rode down the Nespelem to the Columbia and said goodbye on the bluffs overlooking the great river. Men paddled Erskine across the water in a dugout canoe to a wagon, which took him south to the railroad for his return trip to Portland. He meant to visit

Joseph again. But first college and later tuberculosis intervened. By the time Erskine had recovered, Joseph was dead. "That I never saw him again," the 91-year-old Wood wrote in 1970, "still makes me very sad."

In 1896 the Colville reservation agent wrote that the Nez Percés were the only band on the reservation that still wore traditional dress and depended on hunting and gathering to supplement their rations. That year the government opened a day school for native children at Nespelem. At first Joseph discouraged attendance. But he switched to supporting the school after he befriended the teacher and his young daughter, who was able to talk to the chief and translate for him through her knowledge of the Chinook jargon. Joseph visited the school often.

In his second decade at Nespelem, as gold miners and settlers moved in on the Colville reservation, Joseph launched a series of efforts to derail assimilation and to move his people back to the Wallowa country. He traveled far and wide, spanning the continent three times to pursue his cause in every possible venue, from a reservation school room at Nespelem, to a court room in Spokane, to the White House in Washington, D.C.

In 1897 Albert M. Anderson became agent of the Colville reservation and soon fixed his sights on the lone band of "blanket Indians" and their leader. He sent a stream of letters to his superiors, complaining that the Nez Percés "have been persistent in following their ancient traditions and indulging in their primitive customs."

His complaints grew more strident with every year. By 1900 Anderson was outraged that Joseph and the others would not abandon their Nez Percé life and move into houses. "He, with his handful of unworthy followers, prefers the traditional tipi, living on the generosity of the government and passing away their time in a filthy and licentious way of living."

In 1897 Joseph responded to the encroachment of miners and the hostility of his agent by renewing the attempt to move his people to the Wallowa country. Again with the support of Miles and other friends, the chief traveled to Washington, D.C. There Interior Department officials agreed to look into his request. Before returning, Joseph traveled to New York City and rode with Howard and Miles in a parade to the dedication of President Grant's tomb in upper Manhattan.

Joseph at his tipi in Nespelem, Washington, around 1900.
(Courtesy Historical Photograph Collections, Washington
State University)

Joseph attracted a great deal of attention. "The East is
strange to me," he said to one interviewer. "I do not understand
it at all. The green of the trees and the grass is not here. The
quiet of the woods is missing. It is all dirt and noise and hurry
and the people are strange." He marveled at the tall buildings,
trains, elevators and trollies. "In New York it is all wonders,
and I do not understand how the people live."

Joseph stayed at the stately Astor House in Manhattan and
was eagerly sought after by people with an interest in the West
or in Native Americans. One man, who called to remind the
chief of a dinner date, found he had left suddenly. "Chief Joseph
said he wanted to get where he could see some trees," the clerk
told him.

For two years, the government did not act on its promise to
consider Joseph's request. Then, in August of 1899, he received
permission to visit the Wallowa country for the first time in
more than 20 years and see if he could acquire land there. The

country was still remote, with no railroad. It supported a population of about 3,000 people in farming, trades, commerce and intensive cattle raising. The seas of waist-high bunch grass in the valleys were gone, due to heavy grazing. A town called Joseph stood near the lake; the main newspaper in the valley was the *Chieftain*.

Joseph found no support among people in the Wallowa country for his hopes of returning. The government rejected his proposal for living there. Defying Anderson, who forbade him to travel, Joseph went to Washington, D.C., and persuaded officials to reconsider. A year later he visited the Wallowa country again with an Indian inspector, James McLaughlin, hoping the government would back his position. Joseph visited his father's grave and again greeted old friends among the settlers. "There are many white people there now," he wrote with the help of a white friend at Colville. "But I told the inspector I would be satisfied with some land on one side of where there were only a few whites, and where creeks and mountains afford good pasturage."

McLaughlin had spent most of his adult life in the front lines of the government programs for suppressing Native Americans. His recommendation against the return of the Wallowa Nez Percés to their homes was approved in Washington.

Joseph would not give up. He continued to enlist the help of well-known public figures. In 1901 he met Edmond S. Meany, a prominent educator and historian at Washington University. "If the government would only give me a small piece of land for my people in the Wallowa Valley with a teacher that is all I would ask," he wrote the professor, again through a white intermediary.

That summer, Meany visited Joseph at Nespelem. "The interior of Chief Joseph's tipi presents a model appearance of neatness," he wrote. "Indian mats cover the floor and in huge rolls around the edge are buffalo robes now quite scarce among the Indians, and blankets."

> A package wrapped in a buffalo robe was brought to the center of the tipi. It contained a little chest in which was a hundred or more photographs. He knew them all and told of his experiences on the warpath with the soldiers. A little picture he held on one brown palm while he fondly stroked

it with the other. He spoke from his scant supply of English words: "Good woman." Other pictures were shown, but three times he came back to the little one of the "Good woman." Asking to see it, I found written on the back: "To Chief Joseph from his loving daughter, Sarah."

Sarah was Khap-khap-onmi's English name. Joseph said all nine of his children were dead, and he later repeated this in a letter to Meany.

Joseph began another battle in the summer of 1901 when Anderson tried to send the band's children to boarding school in a military barracks at Fort Spokane. The day school at Nespelem was closed. Indian children at Fort Spokane wore white people's clothes and had closely cropped hair. They were forbidden to speak their own languages. Their parents were 75 miles away over rough wagon roads.

Joseph and the parents refused to give up the children. Anderson, claiming that the chief opposed education, cut off all rations and supplies that summer and waited through the fall to starve them out. Joseph traveled to Spokane to meet with a lawyer. Anderson paid informants to track his movements and to spy on deliberations of the Nez Percés. After months of hunger, they gave in. But Joseph continued trying to bring the children back from the boarding school and also tried to have Anderson dismissed.

Anderson was concerned enough about Joseph to spy on him, but in public the agent portrayed Joseph as a broken man. "Joseph is completely cowed and nothing remains of his former fiery spirit," Anderson told a newspaper reporter in June of 1903. The chief "was once a pretty bad Indian, but he is all right now."

Whether or not Joseph's complaints against him had any effect, Anderson was fired later that year and accused, among other things of appointing himself the guardian of Native American orphans and stealing their money. A friendlier and more honest agent took over, and the day school at Nespelem reopened for a time.

This experience could only have increased Joseph's determination to regain his people's home. In 1903 he traveled to Washington, D.C., and New York, meeting with President Theodore Roosevelt and once again seeing his old friend Nelson

This picture of Chief Joseph, by the renowned photographer and Native American historian Edward S. Curtis, was taken in Seattle, Washington, in 1903. (Courtesy Philadelphia Museum of Art: Purchased with funds from the American Museum of Photography)

Miles. He traveled across the country once more in 1904, returning by way of Seattle, where he visited Meany and spoke to students at the university.

"I am an Indian," he told them, "but the same blood that courses through my veins flows through yours."

That fall, as they had for several years, nearly all the Colville Nez Percés left the reservations to work the hop harvest in the Yakima Valley. With the increasing inroads of settlers and miners it was clear that hunting and herding alone would bring diminishing returns and increased dependence on the government.

Joseph was not well, but he made the difficult trip by wagon 75 miles over dirt roads to Fort Spokane to meet the new agent,

John Webster. The chief looked ill and dispirited, Webster wrote, "and complained of always feeling tired."

On the afternoon of September 21, 1904, Joseph's tipi stood in a meadow by the deserted settlement of his people. As he sat inside with his wife, Joseph asked her for his headdress and other ceremonial clothing. He told her, "I may die any time and wish to die as a chieftain."

When she returned with his things from a small hut nearby, Chief Joseph was dead.

He was buried in a temporary grave at Nespelem until the following June, when the Nez Percés held his funeral. Members of the tribe came from Idaho, Montana and Canada. It took 10 interpreters to translate for the large assortment of white and Native American guests on hand. Memorial services were held at other settlements that day across the sprawling Colville

Chief Joseph's grave, Nespelem, Washington. (Photo by Robert Scott)

reservation as the chief was laid to rest in the cemetery at Nespelem.

Professor Meany came from Seattle and with other friends provided a carved granite monument in Joseph's memory. They dug a simple plank coffin out of the temporary grave. His people, following their custom of giving personal witness to the death of a relative or friend, pried the top off and gazed into his face. "Tears fell from the eyes of old warriors, while the widows of the war time gave voice to the wail of the grieving Indian," Meany wrote.

A web of myth shrouded Joseph's lifelong struggle with racism many years before he died. But this myth did not hide Joseph from his own people or their relations across the Northwest. Light in the Mountain, a hero of the war, pointedly welcomed all the guests after Joseph had been buried again.

> I am very glad to meet all you people—that is, the Indians and the whites. When the world was made—we both know the One that made this world. When it was finished, the same One gave man growth.
>
> And out of this land the law was made for both of us, red and white.
>
> And this man, our old chief Joseph, is dead, but then his words are not dead. And for this same reason the law of the soul is the same for both of us.

EPILOGUE

C hief Joseph's people remained at Nespelem after his death. They abandoned efforts to return to the Wallowa country but never moved to the Nez Percé reservation in Idaho, where the treaty of 1863 said they belonged. For this, the government denied them the rights promised in the treaty, including the right to hunt in the Wallowa.

In the early decades of the 1900s Nez Percés of both Nespelem and Idaho who had lived through the war, recorded their story with the help of a sympathetic rancher, Lucullus V. McWhorter. Yellow Wolf, Joseph's nephew, played a large part in preserving this history. He worked with McWhorter over a period of 24 years. Knowing that McWhorter planned to put his words in a book, Yellow Wolf gave the account in the formal oral tradition of his tribe, with two other Nez Percé veterans of the war present at all times to attest to the truth of his words.

"I want the next generation of whites to know and treat the Indian as themselves," he said. "I am telling my story that all may know why the war we did not want [was fought]. War is made to take something not your own."

Like many other Native American groups, the Nez Percés have endured repression, poverty and attempts to exploit their remaining land and resources throughout the 20th century. Only in recent decades have laws such as the one banning Native American religious practices been set aside. Groups attempting to rebuild tribal identity on the reservations still face pressure on their young people to leave the reserves in search of jobs. The fate of some tribes is still uncertain.

The Nez Percés at Nespelem have lived for more than a century now as the smallest of several groups on the Colville reservation. Though mobility and intermarriage have affected them, they still maintain their own identity. In the 1980s they challenged and overturned the state of Oregon's refusal to allow them hunting rights on public land in the Wallowa country. Around that time Joseph's people started to visit their old country to attend the annual fair that white residents had started there, called Chief Joseph Days. Now each year they pitch tipis by the Wallowa River near the town of Joseph and give a great feast. At one of these, in 1990, the people sang a song to their old chief. "He looks back and sees us, laughing and having a good time," said Joe Redthunder, a leader of the Nespelem people.

An irrigation dam at Wallowa Lake has sealed off the salmon spawning areas upstream. But the fish survive in the untamed Imnaha River. They and a handful of other remaining wild salmon stocks in the Northwest face extinction because of power dams on the lower Snake River and because overgrazing and other activities have filled spawning streams with mud. Native American and other groups across the region have mounted a desperate effort to save the salmon, demanding that land and water be used differently so as to protect the fish. They have called for the creation of a new national park to protect the Imnaha and Hells Canyon. Legislation to accomplish this was first introduced in Congress in 1992. In these and in numerous other battles, the collision that began in 1492 in the Caribbean continues today. Joseph remains a towering presence in this struggle.

A well-worn path leads through the Nespelem cemetery to his grave in the powdery earth beneath a small serviceberry tree. Iatowenonmy, his wife, lies beside him. He was raised in his people's traditional school of leadership, with only the power of persuasion—no police, no judges, no jails—to enforce his rule. He learned to seek and cherish harmony among his people and between them and other peoples. Joseph represented his band brilliantly in its confrontation with the seemingly all-powerful society that swept over the continent after 1492. He followed and helped sustain his people through war and waged an unremitting struggle for freedom through years of exile, into the 20th century. He became the advocate and symbol of a different path in the modern world, one that practices kinship and harmony rather than exploitation among all people, and between them and the earth.

SELECTED BIBLIOGRAPHY

DOCUMENTS

Three valuable archive sources are described in the acknowledgments. Some of the most useful primary source material is readily available in books.

Aoki, Haruo. *Nez Perce Oral Narratives*. Berkeley: University of California Press, 1989.
———. *Nez Perce Texts*. Berkeley: University of California Press, 1979.

Both these books provide invaluable insight into Nez Percé culture and language through oral history. They include myths, historic tales and recollections of the speakers. The text is printed in Nez Percé, and in literal translation as well as in conventional English translation. In *Nez Perce Texts* Aoki also provides a sensible analysis of the conflicting versions of Joseph's surrender speech.

Carpenter, Frank D. and Heister Guie and Lucullus V. McWhorter. *Adventures in Geyser Land*. Caldwell, Idaho: Caxton Printers Ltd., 1935. An account of by the tourists who were captured in Yellowstone Park by the Nez Percés.
Chief Joseph. *Chief Joseph's Own Story*. Fairfield, Washington: Ye Galleon Press, 1981. The most widely circulated source of Joseph's own words is this, his speech of 1879 in Washington, D.C., which has been published many times. The Galleon edition is a useful one, including an index and photographs. The translator for this speech was Ad Chapman, an Indian-hating settler who fired the first shot of the war. The text went through one or more editors before it appeared in print. The speech describes a confrontation

between Tuekakas and Henry Spalding that could have happened at the treaty council of 1863, when Spalding was present, and could not have happened at the treaty council of 1855, when he was far away. So in this book I place the confrontation in 1863, rather than 1855 as reported in the speech.

Clark, Ella E. *Indian Legends of the Pacific Northwest*. Berkeley: University of California Press, 1966. Includes several Nez Percé myths, among them the myth of the Seven Devils.

Curtis, Edward S. *The North American Indian*, vol. 8. Norwood, Mass.: 1911. Includes first-person accounts collected by the photographer.

Dunn, Jacob Piatt Jr., *Massacres in the Mountains*. New York: Harper Brothers, 1886.

Drury, Clifford M., ed. *The Diaries and Letters of Henry H. Spalding and Asa Bowen Smith Relating to the Nez Perce Mission, 1838–1842*. Glendale, Ca.: Arthur H. Clark, 1958.

Foster, Ernest Moore. *Pack Train and Transit, First Survey of South Half of Colville Indian Reservation*. Fairfield, Washington: Ye Galleon Press, 1987.

Garcia, Andrew. *Tough Trip Through Paradise*. Sausalito, Ca.: Comstock Editions, 1986. Garcia was a white trader who married Inwholise, a Nez Percé survivor of the war. Years after she died, Garcia recorded his recollection of his wife's account of the war and of the wrenching trip he made with her in search of her father's remains on the war trail in 1879. Coming as it does secondhand from Garcia after many years, Inwholise's account of the war and Joseph's part in it may not be error-free. But it is an important resource. Garcia was himself not friendly toward Joseph because he thought the chief had deliberately taken credit for the deeds of the fighting leaders. It is not likely, therefore, that Garcia, in giving his wife's account, exaggerated Joseph's role.

Gay, Jane E. *With the Nez Perces: Alice Fletcher in the Field 1889–92*. Lincoln: University of Nebraska Press, 1981. The letters of Jane Gay, Fletcher's companion in Idaho, give a revealing portrait of allotment, assimilation and life for the Idaho Nez Percés after the war.

Hines, Donald M. *Tales of the Nez Perce*. Fairfield, Washington: Ye Galleon Press, 1984.

Humphrey, Seth K. *The Indian Dispossessed*. Boston: Little,
Brown, 1906. This includes the most extensive record published of Joseph's debate in 1876 with the commissioners who
ordered his people to abandon the Wallowa country. This is
one of the more important, best authenticated and most
overlooked speeches by Joseph. The translator at the meeting, Perrin Whitman, was one of a few that the Nez Percés
considered reliable. While this and other documents in
Humphrey's book are valuable, his own accounts and inter-
pretations should be ignored.

Irving, Washington. *The Adventures of Captain Louis Eulie
Bonneville*. Boston: Twayne Publishers, 1977.

Johnson, Donald R., ed. *British Establishments on the Columbia and the State of the Fur Trade*. Fairfield, Washington: Ye
Galleon Press, 1981. This document, a report to Congress in
1831, gives detailed information on British activity in the
Northwest and reveals the American attitude toward that
country.

McWhorter, L. V., *Yellow Wolf: His Own Story*. Caldwell,
Idaho: Caxton Printers Ltd., 1986.

———. *Hear Me My Chiefs! Nez Perces History and Legend*.
Caldwell, Idaho: Caxton Printers Ltd., 1986.

These books are indispensable sources of Nez Percé accounts about the war and Joseph's role. Some scholars have
questioned their reliability, but the discrepancies they have
found center on body counts and the course of events in
battle. Whatever mistakes there may be in the Nez Percé
record do not compare with the exaggerations and fabrica-
tions that can be found in many contemporary accounts from
leaders of the army and volunteers in the war.

Sherman, William T. *Travel Accounts of William T. Sherman
to Spokan Falls, Washington Territory, in the Summers of
1877 and 1993*. Fairfield, Washington: Ye Galleon Press,
1984. This is a crucial book, including letters Sherman wrote
to the secretary of war while the general traveled to the West
during the war of 1877. Sherman's own statements are proof
that he and the U.S. government knew, when they ordered
General Gibbon to go after the Nez Percés, that the retreating bands were attacking no one and did not want war.

HISTORIES

Steven Ross Evans's *Chief Joseph and the Red Napoleon Myth*, written in 1969 as a thesis for the history department at Washington State University, is an excellent guide to the historical literature about Joseph. The volumes listed here are important because of the background and analysis they provide.

Bartlett, Grace. *The Wallowa Country 1867–1877*. Fairfield, Washington: Ye Galleon Press, 1984. This is an absolutely indispensable book for anyone interested in Joseph. It shows that conflict with the white settlers of the Wallowa country did not play the main part in driving Joseph's band from its home. Bartlett also provides details unavailable elsewhere about Joseph's conduct and relations with settlers. She quotes many important documents at length or in full and includes maps of the country and of the government's botched reservation plan.

Brown, Mark H. *The Flight of the Nez Perce*. Lincoln: University of Nebraska Press, 1982 (originally published 1967).

Drury, Clifford M. *Henry Harmon Spalding*. Caldwell, Idaho: Caxton Press, 1936.

Gidley, M. *Kopet: A Documentary Narrative of Chief Joseph's Last Years*. Seattle: University of Washington Press, 1981.

Green, Jerome A. *Yellowstone Command: Colonel Nelson A. Miles and the Great Sioux War, 1876–77*. Lincoln: University of Nebraska Press, 1991.

Gulick, Bill. *Chief Joseph Country: Land of the Nez Perce*. Caldwell, Idaho: Caxton Printers Ltd., 1981.

———. *Snake River Country*. Caldwell, Idaho: Caxton Printers Ltd., 1978.

Haines, Francis. *The Nez Perces, Tribesmen of the Columbia Plateau*. Norman: University of Oklahoma Press, 1955.

Howard, Helen Addison. *Saga of Chief Joseph*. Caldwell, Idaho: Caxton Printers Ltd., 1941. Much of the history in this book has been superseded by later studies, but it remains an important source of documents.

Josephy, Alvin M., Jr. *The Nez Perce and the Opening of the Northwest*. New Haven, Conn.: Yale University Press, 1965.

This 700-page book stands as the definitive study of the Nez Percés. A paperback edition is in print, but unfortunately it is abridged.

————. *Now That the Buffalo's Gone, A Study of Today's American Indians*. Norman: University of Oklahoma Press, 1984.

Mark, Joan. *A Stranger in Her Native Land: Alice Fletcher and the Native Indians*. Lincoln: University of Nebraska Press, 1991, paperback.

McDermott, John J. *Forlorn Hope: The Battle of White Bird Canyon and the Beginning of the Nez Perce War*. Boise: Idaho State Historical Society, 1978.

McLaughlin, James. *My Friend the Indian*. Lincoln: University of Nebraska Press, 1989. McLauchlin's accounts of Joseph are biased and unreliable. The book is a profile of the self-deception practiced by many of those who tried to eradicate Native American cultures.

Newman, Peter C. *Caesars of the Northwest, the Story of the Hudson's Bay Company*. New York: Viking Penguin, 1987.

Ronda, James P. *Astoria and Empire*. Lincoln: University of Nebraska Press, 1990.

Schwantes, Carlos A. *The Pacific Northwest: An Interpretive History*. Lincoln: University of Nebraska Press, 1989, paperback.

Slickpoo, Allen P., So. *Noon-Nee-Me-Poo: Nez Perce Culture and History*. Lapwaii, Idaho: The Nez Perce Tribe, 1973.

Stevenson, Elmo. *Nature Rambles in the Wallowas*. Enterprise, Oregon: Pika Press, 1985. Originally published in 1937, this gives a delightful overview of the geography and plant and animal life of the Wallowa Mountains.

Trafzer, Clifford E., ed. *Northwestern Tribes in Exile*. Sacramento: Sierra Oaks Publishing Co., 1987.

Walker, Deward E., Jr. *Conflict and Schism in Nez Perce Acculturation: A Study of Religion and Politics*. Moscow: University of Idaho Press, 1985. This is a study of the Idaho Nez Percés in the postwar period and into the 20th century. The book, though laced with jargon that makes it less than readable, gives an important viewpoint and information on the persistence of Nez Percé culture.

Wilfong, Cheryl. *Following the Nez Perce Trail*. Corvallis: Oregon State University Press, 1990. This book, which concentrates on the war period, includes a large collection of documentary excerpts and photographs.

Wood, Erskine. *Days with Chief Joseph*. Portland: Oregon Historical Society, 1970.

MAPS

Excellant maps are essential to comprehend the great landscape on which Joseph lived and struggled. The shaded relief maps of the late Erwin Raisz (Raisz Landform Maps; PO Box 2254; Jamaica Plain, MA 02310) are detailed yet vivid. His *Landforms of the Northwestern States* (1941) is especially useful.

For a more detailed focus on the homeland of the Nez Percés showing developments to the present day, see the standard one-by-two degree quadrangle maps of the U.S. Geological Survey (Map Distribution; Box 25286, Federal Center; Denver, CO 80225); The Grangeville map (45116-A1) includes the Wallowa country. The rest of the area is covered in Pullman (46116-A1), Hamilton (46114-A1) and Elk City (45114-A1). For stunning photography of the region see the books by Bill Gulick cited above.

Bartlett, Josephy and Wilfong, all cited above, include useful line-drawing maps dealing with the history of the Nez Percés and the war.

INDEX

Italic numbers indicate illustrations.